FOR THE LOVE OF

A COLLECTOR'S GUIDE

HOLLY STOWE

PUBLICATIONS INTERNATIONAL, LTD.

Holly Stowe is an avid Beanie Babies collector and writer. Her Beanie Babies articles have appeared in various publications and magazines including *Beanie Mania* and *Beanie Collector*. She is the author of *The Complete Idiot's Guide to Beanie Babies*.

Photography by Brian Warling/Brian Warling Photography.

Pictured on front cover: top: Flutter the butterfly (see page 34); bottom, left to right: Pinky the flamingo (see page 60), Ants the anteater (see page 15), Quackers the duck (see page 63), Smoochy the frog (see page 72), Bubbles the fish (see page 21), Inky the octopus (see page 44), Daisy the cow (see page 27), Peace the bear (see page 58). Pictured on back cover: Beak the kiwi bird (see page 17) and Princess the bear (see page 61).

Acknowledgments:
Special thanks to the generous collectors who loaned their Beanie Babies collections for this book: Lindsay Gehrls; Kelley Hardman; Cheryl Damato; Frank Magos; Diana Petersen and her generous customer, Judy, with Diana Petersen Collectibles at 1452 Miner Street, Des Plaines, IL 60016, 847/296-6335; Marianna and Dominic Stocco; Rachel Kagan; Leah Benjamin; and Jan Schroeder.

ISBN 0-7853-3987-6

Contents

Beanie Babies Collecting Tips

THE BEANIE EXPLOSION

The craze over Beanie Babies is about as far-reaching as any you'll ever see. People from all walks of life collect Beanies. Some collect to make money on the secondary market, some as an investment, and some simply for the love of these little "babies." Whatever your reason for collecting, you are not alone.

THE HISTORY OF TY, INC.

So how did this all get started?

In 1962, H. Ty Warner, a recent graduate of Kalamazoo College, went to work for Dakin, Inc., a well-known manufacturer of stuffed animals. Warner worked for Dakin for the next 18 years. In 1986, he settled in the western suburbs of Chicago, near Oak Brook, where he started Ty, Inc., setting out to do what he had done for years with Dakin: produce stuffed animals.

BEANIE BABIES ARE BORN

Warner came up with a design and marketing strategy for a child-sized toy that would be within a child-sized budget. Thus, the original nine Beanie Babies—Spot the dog (spotless), Squealer the pig, Patti the platypus, Pinchers (Punchers) the lobster, Chocolate the moose, Flash the dolphin, Splash the whale, Cubbie (Brownie) the bear, and Legs the frog—were presented at a toy convention in late 1993. They were introduced to the world in January 1994. Six months later, 25 new Beanies made their appearance.

The marketing strategy? The basis of all economics: supply and demand. To limit availability (supply), and keep the product flow and prices somewhat regulated, Ty, Inc., chose to distribute Beanie Babies through a network of specialty stores rather than larger chains. To create demand, Ty worked out a schedule of "planned obsolescence." A certain number of times each year, some Beanies would be retired while new ones were issued.

As with most things, the frenzy didn't happen overnight, nor was the entire country taken by storm. The eye of the storm was, naturally, the Chicago area, Ty, Inc.'s home turf. But it took two years or more for the storm to really develop even there. By the latter part of 1996, the storm was a full-blown tornado with gusts reaching across the country.

TEENIE BEANIES

Then...April 11, 1997. McDonald's started a new Happy Meal promotion, issuing Teenie Beanies for ten Beanie Babies. Planned as a five-week promotion with two Teenies to be featured each week, McDonald's was forced to call a halt after only ten days because all five weeks' worth of Teenies were gone. Some stores sold out in the first weekend! All this in spite of the fact that McDonald's, realizing they had underestimated demand, did very little advertising for the promotion. For the second Happy Meal Teenie Beanie promotion, which began on May 22, 1998, McDonald's ordered twice the production of each Teenie Beanie. But once again, the Teenies sold out in most McDonald's stores by the end of the first weekend. The third Teenie Beanie bonanza came in May 1999, and the popular Teenie International Bears followed in June. It seems likely that Teenies will become an annual event for the foreseeable future.

BEANIE BUDDIES

In the fall of 1998, Ty introduced a new line of plush toys, called Beanie Buddies, based on the Beanie Babies styles. Among the first Buddies announced were a royal blue Peanut the elephant, Humphrey the camel, and cranberry Teddy, thus giving Beanie collectors the opportunity to add at least a variation of the older, expensive Beanies to their collections. As with the Beanie Babies, the Beanie Buddies are also subject to a schedule of "planned obsolescence." Twigs the giraffe was the first Buddy to retire.

BEANIES ONLINE

The Internet has played no small part in the incredible Beanie Baby craze. In August 1996, Ty opened its own Web site (http://www.ty.com) to promote its entire line of toys, but the focus of the site was, of course, on Beanie Babies. A site called Beaniemom's Net Letter contains a weekly updated pricing guide on retired pieces; nationwide swap meet and trade listings that are updated almost daily; and information on important news

5 GREAT BEANIE WEB SITES

1. Ty, Inc.: http://www.ty.com
2. Beaniemom's Net Letter: http://www.beaniemom.com
3. Beaniholics: http://www.geocities.com/Heartland/Park/4116/
4. Beaniemania: http://www.beaniemania.net/
5. eBay Auctions: http://www.ebay.com/

items such as counterfeits, promotions, and fundraisers. Many online auctions and trading boards exist as well, but be careful when trading online. Make sure you get references and read hints about Beanie transactions on the Internet.

The Internet has been a driving force in the prices of Beanies—especially retired Beanies, but also currents and hard-to-finds. Ty has long been concerned about pricing and the secondary market, and the company has taken steps to try to keep retail prices down and to attempt to slow, if not stop, the sale of Beanies by retailers to secondary dealers. Ty's stand underlines its commitment to keeping Beanies primarily as a children's toy.

DETERMINING VALUE

Beanie prices are based on a Beanie that is in mint condition with mint tags. The Beanie's tags, especially its hang tags, are actually worth about 50 percent of the Beanie's value, though the tag more greatly affects the value of the recently retired Beanies. Many of the older Beanies were retired before the frenzy began, and people didn't concern themselves with the condition of the tag. The oldest Beanies are rare enough that many devoted collectors are happy to have one with or without a tag. (Tagless Beanies are often more affordable, as well!)

More-recent retireds, especially those from October 1997 and later, are easily found in mint condition with mint tags. On these Beanies, even a slight crease or bend in the tag can mean a decrease in value of 10 to 40 percent. A Beanie with a heavily creased or mangled hang tag may be considered to have about the same value as a Beanie with no tag at all.

There are currently five generations of hang (also called "swing") tags. These are the heart-shaped tags attached to the Beanie's ear with a plastic connector. The older the generation of hang tag, the more valuable the Beanie. There is no hard-and-fast rule about just how much an older hang tag adds to the value, but, as a general guideline, first-generation hang tags currently add $200 to $300 to the going price of *the most recent version* of the Beanie. Second-generation tags add $100 to $200; third-generation tags add $50 to $100. Fourth-generation tags are readily available, so they don't add much to the value. Redesigned Beanies are often an exception to this rule, as is the case with the tie-dye Batty.

Another exception belongs to Beanies who have been redesigned and released with the same hang tag found on the previous version. For example, the tie-dyed version of Lizzy the lizard came with a third-generation hang tag but was redesigned as the blue/black Lizzy. A third-generation tag from a blue/black Lizzy could increase the value of tie-dyed Lizzy significantly, and, as a result, she will be valued more highly than if her tag solely belonged to that variation.

Which, of course, brings us to the ethics of "retagging" Beanies. Technically, once a Beanie has been altered in any way from the way it left the factory, it's not considered to be in truly mint condition. That includes even removing the tag and the connector from the Beanie's ear

and replacing it intact later. Beanies should only be retagged with tags with which they were originally released, and when a Beanie is sold, any retagging should be disclosed to the buyer.

To protect yourself on the secondary market, make sure you know which Beanies came with which tags, and make sure the tush tag matches the hang tag as well. Unfortunately, there are unethical people who will try to make a buck by faking a "more valuable" tag.

Collectors should also note that while there was a time when Beanies with the wrong tags were uncommon, those days are over. Mistags, even tush tags with the wrong names, are fairly common. Over 1,400 different mistags had been noticed at last count. A few mistags—those that affect an entire production run—are considered "classic," but don't get caught up in paying extra for a Beanie just because it doesn't have its own tag. Remember that hang tags are easily switched and not necessarily a factory error to begin with.

CLASSIC MISTAGS

Quacker instead of Quackers
Spook instead of Spooky
Tuck instead of Tusk
Sparky with a Dotty tush tag
Echo and Waves with each others' hang and tush tags

HANG TAGS

There are five generations of hang tags. You may have only seen the fourth- or fifth-generation hang tags. All of the hang tags are heart shaped; they are primarily red with gold foil edging; and all have the name "ty" on the front in white.

First-Generation Hang Tags

This is the tag that was on the original nine Beanies as well as a few others that came out early in Beanie history. The heart shape is a little shorter from top to bottom than later tags, and the hole for

the connector is at the side of the tag rather than in the upper corner. This tag is not folded over like the other generations. The "ty" lettering on the front is skinny, and the yellow star found on fourth- and fifth-generation tags has not yet appeared. The back of the tag features the Beanie name and style number as well as the company information.

Second-Generation Hang Tags

The second-generation hang tag shares its proportions with the first tag. The "ty" on the front is still skinny, but now the hole for the connector is in the

upper left corner of the heart, and the tag is folded over like a book cover. The company information has been moved to the inside left. The inside right of the tag acts as a gift tag, with the words "to," "from," and "with love." The back of the tag says "retain tag for reference." This style tag was in use until early- to mid-1995.

Third-Generation Hang Tags

This tag was referred to as "old tag" until recently, because by the time most Beanie collectors jumped on the boat, fourth-generation tags were already in use. Many of these collectors didn't even realize there were two incarnations of tags before the third-generation tag!

This tag was used from mid-1995 to mid-

1996. The heart is slightly more square, and the "ty" lettering on the front has fattened up and is now referred to as the "bubble" Ty. The insides and back of the tag haven't changed significantly.

Fourth-Generation Hang Tags

The most widely found of the surviving hang tags is the fourth-generation tag, introduced in mid-1996 with the Righty, Lefty, Libearty, and Maple releases. (These four Beanies were among the summer 1996 releases that never had third-generation tags.) Many changes were found on the fourth-generation tags, starting with the appearance of a yellow star on the front.

Within the star are the words "BEANIE ORIGINAL BABY." The "ty" on the front is no longer edged in gold. The inside left of the tag still contains the company information, but the right side is very different. Each Beanie now has a birthday and, instead of the "to/from" area, a poem telling a little bit about the Beanie's personality. On the bottom of the inside right, Ty invites people to visit their Web site.

Fifth-Generation Hang Tags

The fifth-generation hang tag came at the same time as the release of the January 1998 "newbeans." At first glance, the tag is almost identical to the fourth-generation tag. The primary difference between the two is a change in the typeface used. The style

number has been dropped from the inside (though it still appears in the bar code on the back of the tag), and the Beanie's birthday is now spelled out rather than in numeric form. "The Beanie Babies Collection" has a ® mark, and the Web site information has been shortened.

TUSH TAGS

If only the tush tags were as easy to differentiate as the hang tags are! Fortunately, some of the changes in tush tags have been minor and are not considered a separate generation. The very first tush tags were black and white with four lines of lettering. The lettering ran the long way on the tag rather than across it, as it does on the red-and-white tush tags. There was no Ty heart. All the four-line, black-and-white tush tags have 1993 copyright dates. These appear only on "pre-Beanie Beanies" like Brownie, Punchers, and the deep-fuchsia Patti.

First-Generation Tush Tags

Still in black and white and in use until midway through the third-generation hang tags, the first-generation tush tag has five lines of printing and either 1993 or 1995 copyright dates. The name "Beanie Babies" doesn't appear on the tag.

Second-Generation Tush Tags

Late in 1995 or early in 1996, Ty changed the tush tag dramatically. Now white with red ink, the tush tag bears the Ty heart on one side (still no mention of the name "Beanie Babies") and consumer information and copyright dates on the other. (It's interesting to note that Beanies that have a "recycled" style number keep the copyright date of their predecessor.)

Third-Generation Tush Tags

The next incarnation of tush tag was born when the fourth-generation hang tags came along in mid-1996. The words "The Beanie Baby Collection," with a ™

to indicate trademark, are found above the Ty heart on the red-and-white tag, and the Beanie's name appears below the heart. The tag itself and the printing are smaller than the previous generation. In mid-1997, clear stickers started appearing over the Ty hearts with a small red star in the upper left corner. These stickers were a transition into the next generation.

Fourth-Generation Tush Tags

Essentially the same as the third tag, the fourth generation features a small red star printed above and to the left of the Ty heart. This tush tag began appearing in early fall 1997.

Fifth-Generation Tush Tags

Still essentially the same tag as its predecessor, the fifth-generation tush tag began appearing in late fall 1997. The Beanie's name now shows a small ™, and there is also a ® mark after the words "Beanie Babies" in "The Beanie Babies Collection."

Sixth-Generation Tush Tags

Around the time fifth-generation hang tags appeared, sixth-generation tush tags came out. The only difference is that now the entire phrase "The Beanie Babies Collection" is registered. Many collectors consider the differences among the fourth- through sixth-generation tush tags so slight that they could easily be considered one generation.

Seventh-Generation Tush Tags

With the January 1999 releases, a new generation of tush tags arrived. In an effort to stop counterfeits, Ty put a hologram of the Ty heart logo on the top of the tush tag. On the reverse side, a light red heart is printed. This heart is heat-sensitive: If you hold your finger over it, the image disappears. It does return once it has cooled down.

PROTECTING YOURSELF AGAINST COUNTERFEITS

Counterfeit Beanies have become more and more of a problem over time. To protect yourself from unknowingly spending money on counterfeits, really study the tags. And, as mentioned previously, make sure you know what year your Beanie was copyrighted. Another good idea is to try to find one that you're sure is the real thing (such as at a Ty retailer), and compare. For people with access to the Internet, the Beaniemom Web site maintains a page devoted to counterfeit Beanies and a list of potential traits of various counterfeits. If in doubt, remember the old saying: If it sounds too good to be true, it probably is. Buyers should always try to buy from Ty retailers or from someone with good references.

USING THIS GUIDE

What goes into determining whether a Beanie is a good investment, a recommended, or a highly recommended? For the serious Beanie collector, it's obvious that every older retired (prior to January 1, 1997) is highly recommended, but the current prices on these Beanies make them out of reach for most people. Unless you are driven to having every Beanie, your best bet is to look at more-recent retireds. The vast majority will never obtain the level of the older retireds simply because there are more of them available, but these are the Beanies that are more within the reach of the average collector.

So, instead of aiming for the older and more rare Beanies, focus on spreading out your investment with Beanies that may

not even be retired yet but have a bright future. These include any of the Beanie bears, which are by far the most popular Beanie group, as well as any of the Beanies that have Teenie Beanie and Beanie Buddy counterparts. Recently retired Beanies are also recommended, but don't rush to buy one just after it retires. The trend in prices has been a significant increase just after a retirement, followed by a drop (or "correction") about six weeks after an announcement. Thus, six weeks after a retirement announcement is a great time to pick up the Beanies you don't have in your collection. Prices generally stay lower until the next retirement.

This guide lists currents, even hard-to-find currents, at the going retail price of $5–7. You don't need to be the first on your block to have a new or hard-to-find Beanie, and you will be well rewarded for having patience. Even if a Beanie retires quickly, as was the case with the 1997 Teddy and Snowball, you're better off spending your money knowing the Beanie is retired than trying to buy it for a premium price. Otherwise, you're taking a chance that the Beanie may be out for years, becoming as common as any other Beanie.

All markets, be they stocks or Beanies, have price corrections and points of resistance. The trick is to find a pattern to the corrections and use it to your advantage. Beanies haven't been around long enough to show a sure pattern. This uncertainty is helping to feed the Beanie market right now. As for collecting, always follow the primary rule: Don't collect anything you don't like. That way, whatever happens to the market, you will always have something you can enjoy.

1997 TEDDY `HIGHLY RECOMMENDED`

The 1997 Teddy resembles the new-faced brown Teddy, but his fur is more caramel-colored than brown. When a picture of this little bear first appeared on the Ty Web site, he had green and red bows on his neck, but collectors will usually find him wearing the red scarf with white fringe shown at right. The 1997 Teddy was retired on December 31, 1997, after only three months in Beaniedom. Given the short amount of time he remained on the market and the fact he was retired before many collectors were able to find him, his value should increase tremendously.

Born 12/25/96 • Released 10/1/97 • Retired 12/31/97 •
Estimated Value: ♥4 $40

1998 TEDDY `HIGHLY RECOMMENDED`

This little white holiday bear is dotted with green holly leaves and red berries; thus, it's no surprise he has come to be known by collectors as simply "Holly." Like his 1997 twin (pictured above), 1998 Teddy wears a Santa cap—but his is made from the same holly material as his body and trimmed in red. As an extra surprise, the 1998 Teddy rings in with bells on—he has a tiny little bell hidden inside the end of his cap! Given the history of the 1997 Teddy, it came as no surprise to collectors when Ty retired this little bear at the end of the '98 holiday season.

Born 12/25/98 • Released 9/30/98 • Retired 12/31/98 • Estimated Value: ♥5 $40

1999 Signature Bear

Be sure to sign yourself up to find one of these beautiful bears. In this picture, he appears to be a nice taupe color, but up close you can see that his plush is really made from two different colors of threads, a taupe and a light gray. That embroidered red heart on his chest features the embroidered signature of Ty Warner himself, and his ribbon is burgundy edged with white. Like the Class of 1998's Wise the owl (pictured on page 89), the Signature Bear is likely to be retired at the end of the year.

Born n/a • Released 1/1/99 • Current • Estimated Value: ⑤ $5–7

Ally the Alligator   HIGHLY RECOMMENDED

Avocado Ally appeared with the second release of Beanies and was never redesigned during his time as a current. The brown-on-green spots you see on Ally's back are also found on Speedy the turtle (see page 75). It's extremely difficult to find intact first- and second-generation hang tags on Ally, probably because children loved to play with him from the get-go. Devoted Beanie collectors covet him all the same—mint tags, beat-up tags, or no tags! Due to his long reign as a current, Ally can be found fairly easily on the secondary market, so now is a good time to pick him up at a reasonable price.

Born 3/14/94 • Released 6/25/94 • Retired 10/1/97 • Estimated Value: ❶ $250
❷ $150   ❸ $80   ❹ $40

ALMOND THE BEAR

Collectors will be nutty for this new Beanie bear design, released in April 1999, that features longer and floppier legs than the previous lay-down style seen on Cubbie (page 26) and Sammy (page 67). Almond is beige, as you would guess, and his long legs end at the bottoms of his paws in cream with embroidered toes. As you can see, the new-style bear has small rounded ears, a black plastic nose, and an embroidered mouth.

Born 4/14/99 • Released 4/19/99 • Current • Estimated Value: ❺ $5–7

AMBER THE GOLD TABBY

Amber's body style was first seen in January 1999 with the release of Scat the cat (see page 68). This orange-striped tabby with cream-colored paws and embroidered toes is a purr-fect addition to the cat family. With cream-colored plush accents and pink nose, mouth, and whiskers, Amber is the cat's meow.

Born 2/21/99 • Released 4/20/99 • Current • Estimated Value: ❺ $5–7

ANTS THE ANTEATER RECOMMENDED

Ants very closely resembles the retired Beanie Baby, Tank the armadillo (see page 81), especially the second version of Tank with nine lines and no shell. These two Beanies share the same gray plush, and they're both long and—well—tanklike, as shown in the photo at right. When Ants was introduced in May 1998, many collectors were skeptical about the desirability of a Beanie anteater; however, when seen up close he's as cute as a bug in a rug. TEENIE BEANIE (THIRD SET)

Born 11/7/97 • Released 5/30/98 • Retired 3/31/99 • Estimated Value: ❺ $7

BALDY THE EAGLE RECOMMENDED

On Baldy's original release on May 11, 1996, his name was printed in all capital letters on the inside of his fourth-generation hang tag. (This error was also found on Tuffy the terrier and Claude the crab in the May 11, 1997, release.) Baldy, with his coal-black plush and gleaming white head, was the first of the professional-basketball Beanies. He was featured in a special promotion in conjunction with the NBA's Philadelphia 76ers in January 1998. Being our national symbol, Baldy fit in perfectly in the City of Brotherly Love. Retired after less than a year, Baldy may become one of the more valuable May 1998 retirees.

Born 2/17/96 • Released 5/11/97 • Retired 5/1/98 • Estimated Value: ❹ $14 ❺ $12

BATTY THE BAT HIGHLY RECOMMENDED (TIE-DYE VERSION)

The second bat in the Beanie Babies line, Batty was a fitting replacement for the retired Radar (page 63). With his wings wrapped around him, Batty becomes one of the smallest Beanies around. The original version of Batty featured a pinkish-brown plush (see photo, left), but in fall 1998, he flew into stores wearing deep jewel-toned tie-dye with a dark brown nose and feet. This Beanie's most interesting feature is the Velcro hook-and-loop fasteners on the tips of his wings. The Velcro allows Batty to be wrapped around another Beanie or

strapped on a child's wrist like a bracelet. Despite many people's feelings of distaste toward bats, Batty has proved extremely popular—probably due to his unusual wings and, now, the beautiful tie-dye.

Pinkish-brown: Born 10/29/96 • Released 10/1/97 • Retired 3/31/99 • Estimated Value: ❹ $10
❺ $8 Tie-dye: Born 10/29/96 • Released October '98 (approximate) • Retired 3/31/99 •
Estimated Value: ❺ $20

BEAK THE KIWI BIRD

This fuzzy bird is native to New Zealand. Unlike most birds, kiwis in real life have very small wings. Beak's nappy tie-dyed brown plush is not sculpted like that of some of the other napped Beanies. As you can see, Beak's distinguishing feature is, of course, his long narrow beak, which helps him stand out from the crowd. This bird flew onto retailers' shelves in September 1998. **BEANIE BUDDY**

Born 2/3/98 • Released 9/30/98 • Current • Estimated Value: ❺ $5–7

BERNIE THE ST. BERNARD `HIGHLY RECOMMENDED`

Bernie is a member of the Beanie dogs—one of the most popular Beanie "groups." Bernie (along with Doby the Doberman, page 29) was among the second release of purebreds—dogs who carry their breed as part of their name. Many of the previous releases, such as Spot (page 77) and Rover (page 67), didn't belong to any specific breed. This somewhat sad-looking pup is still reasonable in price.

Born 10/3/96 • Released 1/1/97 • Retired 9/22/98 • Estimated Value: ❹ $9 ❺ $8

BESSIE THE COW `HIGHLY RECOMMENDED`

Bessie has had two different colors of horns: The horns on the earlier Bessies were a little darker than the horns on the more recent Bessies. Pictured at right is the lighter-horned version. Even though Bessie had been around since June 1995, her retirement in October 1997 caught many collectors by surprise. Daisy, the black cow, had been out a year longer, so most expected Daisy (page 27) to be sent out to pasture first. As a result, many collectors still need Bessie to complete their collections, and her value has increased more than that of the average Beanie. Notice anything odd about Bessie's birthday? It's after her release date!

Born 6/27/95 • Released 6/3/95 • Retired 10/1/97 • Estimated Value: ❸ $85 ❹ $45

BLACKIE THE BEAR `RECOMMENDED`

When Blackie's friend Cubbie (page 26) retired, Blackie was left as the only remaining lay down–style bear. We knew he probably wouldn't be far behind in joining the rest of his ilk in the forest of retirement. Released in the summer of 1994, Blackie was current for four long years—positively geriatric in Beanie terms!—so, though his value will certainly increase, don't expect miracles. Blackie, with his coal-black plush and brown plush snout, was one of the group of Beanies shipped in January 1998 whose fifth-generation hang tags had the word "original" spelled "origiinal" on the front and had the "r" left out of "surface" on the back. Look for these errors on the bunny trio of Floppity, Hippity, and Hoppity (pages 34, 41, and 43, respectively), as well as on Curly, Peace, and Valentino the bears (pages 27, 58, and 86).

Born 7/15/94 • Released 6/25/94 • Retired 9/15/98 • Estimated Value: ❶ $250 ❷ $150 ❸ $75 ❹ $8 ❺ $7

BLIZZARD THE TIGER `HIGHLY RECOMMENDED`

So many rumors! Ever since Ty had to change Doodle's name to Strut because of a potential trademark infringement, collectors were convinced that Blizzard would be retired in October 1997. Therefore, she became very hard to find. At one point, there were even pictures distributed of Blizzard with a "Snowball" hang tag, but those turned out to be forgeries. Finally, the predictions came true on May 1, 1998, when the tiger-striped, pink-nosed Blizzard was retired, but it's hard to say whether her retirement was caused by trademark problems, or if it was simply Ty's decision.

Born 12/12/96 • Released 5/11/97 • Retired 5/1/98 • Estimated Value: ❹ $11 ❺ $10

BONES THE DOG RECOMMENDED

Bones was the second Beanie Babies dog to be released. (Spot, featured on page 77 and one of the original nine Beanies, was the first.) Most people think Bones is just a mutt, but, as you can see, it's likely he's modeled after a Bloodhound with his tan plush and long brown ears and tail. Bones is the Beanie everyone thinks of as being a "Pound Puppy," from the popular children's toy series that appeared several years before Beanies were introduced to the world. Teenie Bones was featured in the second McDonald's collection. His Teenie namesake will help his value over time. TEENIE BEANIE (SECOND SET)

Born 1/18/94 • Released 6/25/94 • Retired 5/1/98 • Estimated Value: ❤1 $250
❤2 $150 ❤3 $75 ❤4 $10 ❤5 $10

BONGO THE MONKEY RECOMMENDED

Bongo was originally released with the name Nana. Nana is one of the rarest Beanies around. Some Bongos were Nanas once upon a time until "Bongo" was taped over "Nana" on the tag! As shown here, Bongo was released with a tan tail and a brown tail. The tag generation, along with the tail color, is what affects his value. TEENIE BEANIE (SECOND SET), BEANIE BUDDY

Nana: Born n/a • Released 6/3/95 • Retired (unknown) • Estimated Value: ❤3 $3,000
Brown-tailed Bongo: Born 8/17/95 • Released 2/6/96 • Retired 6/29/96 • Estimated Value: ❤3 $100
❤4 $50 Tan-tailed Bongo: Born 8/17/95 • Released 6/3/95 • Retired 12/31/98 •
Estimated Value: ❤3 $75 ❤4 $8 ❤5 $7

BRITANNIA THE BEAR HIGHLY RECOMMENDED

ritannia is one of the "patriotic" Beanies. With a Union Jack embroidered on her chest, she is available only in the United Kingdom, making her very desirable to collectors in the United States. If her flag is missing, it's hard to tell whether it's Teddy the new-faced brown bear or Britannia. The bear pictured at left is obviously Britannia! TEENIE INTERNATIONAL BEAR

Born 12/15/97 • Released 12/31/97 • Current • Estimated Value: 5 $10–15

BRONTY THE BRONTOSAURUS RECOMMENDED

oor Bronty! Released too early and retired too soon to have a birthday or a poem, his blue tie-dyed plush (the same as Sting the stingray's, page 78) makes up for this slight. Every Bronty is just a little different. The Bronty pictured here is mainly blue, with just a hint of green. A mint-condition Bronty commands a premium price. An interesting fact: Bronty shares a style number with Righty the elephant (featured on page 65).

Born n/a • Released 6/3/95 • Retired 6/15/96 • Estimated Value: 3 $650

BRUNO THE TERRIER RECOMMENDED

hen brutish Bruno was first released, his picture didn't do him justice (see photo at left). A lot of people didn't think much of him until he started appearing in stores, at which point people soon clamored to take the cute pup home. Bruno has a long, rounded, brown-and-white nose and solid, muscular-looking body. Collectors were stunned when Bruno was retired in September 1998, just 9 1/2 months after his release. Look for his secondary-market value to be strong, given his short life as a current.

Born 9/9/97 • Released 12/31/97 • Retired 9/18/98 • Estimated Value: 5 $7

BUBBLES THE FISH `RECOMMENDED`

With her bold black-and-yellow stripes, it's no wonder Bubbles's name is similar to Bumble the bee's (see below). Bubbles was the second of the fish trio (Coral, page 25, and Goldie, page 38, are the other fish) to be retired. She swam into the Beanie pond at the same time as Coral but, unlike Coral, was around after the Teenie Beanies reeled in countless new Beanie collectors. Beware of Bubbles bearing a Grunt tush tag! Chances are it's a counterfeit. **BEANIE BUDDY**

Born 7/2/95 • Released 6/3/95 • Retired 5/11/97 • Estimated Value: ❸ $160 ❹ $100

BUCKY THE BEAVER `HIGHLY RECOMMENDED`

Nobody knows exactly what prompted the retirement of this toothy Beanie. Bucky shares the same basic body shape with Ringo the racoon (page 65), Sly the fox (page 71), and Stinky the skunk (page 79), and some collectors figured Ty thought that was too many Beanies with the same shape. Others thought it was because Bucky was one of the less-popular Beanies. If that's true, Bucky may turn out to be a great investment for those just starting to collect retireds because of his still-inexpensive price. Now may be a good time to pick him up!

Born 6/8/95 • Released 1/7/96 • Retired 12/31/97 • Estimated Value: ❸ $80 ❹ $25

BUMBLE THE BEE `RECOMMENDED`

Bumble, one of the smallest Beanies, can fit easily into the palm of your hand. The yellow-and-black Bumble, shown at left, is the only Beanie from the June 15, 1996, retirement that was shipped with fourth-generation hang tags and a poem. Don't be fooled if someone tells you the older tag is worth more money on this little bee: This is the only Beanie on which a fourth-generation tag is actually more valuable than a third-generation tag.

Born 10/16/95 • Released 6/3/95 • Retired 6/15/96 • Estimated Value: ❸ $350 ❹ $425

BUTCH THE BULL TERRIER

With Bruno the terrier's retirement, Butch has come along to become the Big Dog on Campus. Butch's plush is white, but he has a patch of brown plush on his right eye and a wavy brown spot reminiscent of Daisy the cow and Spot the dog (pages 27 and 77, respectively). As you can see, Butch has a long Roman nose and pointed ears just like a real bull terrier. As a member of the popular dog family, he's sure to be favored by collectors.

Born 10/2/98 • Released 1/1/99 • Current • Estimated Value: 5 $5–7

CANYON THE COUGAR

Canyon's tan plush is accented by his white belly, black-and-white ears, and a white muzzle with a strip of black plush (shown at right). His nose is large and pink. Cougars are the largest of the small wild cat family and live primarily in the mountains of the western United States, but Canyon can be found on collectors' shelves around the world.

Born 5/29/98 • Released 9/30/98 • Current • Estimated Value: 5 $5–7

CAW THE CROW `RECOMMENDED`

Because of Caw's bright orange beak and webbed feet, he is often referred to as a "black duck." This crow isn't very well known outside of Beanie collecting circles. Lucky collectors may be able to find him at a flea market or a garage sale, even without a hang tag, for much less than his going value. The Korean-made Caws are often much plumper than Caws made in China, which is where most Beanies are made. Caw doesn't carry quite as high a price tag as some of the other, older retireds.

Born n/a • Released 6/3/95 • Retired 6/15/96 • Estimated Value: 3 $375

CHEEKS THE BABOON

Cheeks is one of the wildest Beanie Babies you'll see. As this picture shows, his face is what sets him apart from the crowd: His long nose has a stripe of red plush, and on either side you'll see the same black-and-white striped plush that Jabber the parrot has around his eyes (see page 45). As if all this crazy detail weren't enough, collectors need only look at his backside for another surprise!

Born 5/18/99 • Released 4/17/99 • Current • Estimated Value: ❺ $5–7

CHILLY THE POLAR BEAR RECOMMENDED

Chilly was one of the first Beanies to increase substantially in value. As an early Beanie, he was a favorite toy for many children before Beanies became collectible. He's very difficult to find in anything close to mint condition because, like all the white plush Beanies, he gets dirty very easily. In pristine condition as seen here, Chilly is a gorgeous, gleaming Beanie. Along with Blackie (page 18), Peking (page 59), and Cubbie (page 26), he is one of the lay down–style bears. Chilly's style number was reused on the also-all-white Flip the cat (page 34). BEANIE BUDDY

Born n/a • Released 6/25/94 • Retired 1/7/96 • Estimated Value: ❶ $1,500 ❷ $1,300 ❸ $1,100

CHIP THE CALICO CAT RECOMMENDED

Calico cats, like Chip, are almost always female. The genes that make cats calico are part of the same genes that make cats female. The Beanie Babies cat group generally follows the Beanie dogs in popularity, but since Ty has released fewer cats than dogs in the Beanie family, any new cat is considered a "must-have." The black, gold, and white Chip was very hard to find when she was first released. TEENIE BEANIE (THIRD SET), BEANIE BUDDY

Born 1/26/96 • Released 5/1/97 • Retired 3/31/99 • Estimated Value: ❹ $7 ❺ $7

CHOCOLATE THE MOOSE RECOMMENDED

Chocolate was one of the original nine Beanies introduced in January 1994, and is "mom" to one of the original McDonald's Teenie Beanies. Chocolate's clever name made him extremely popular among older collectors. Young collectors just love the floppy orange antlers and "bemoosed" expression evident in the photo at right. On Canadian Chocolates with a fourth-generation hang tag, check to see if the word "moose" appears as the typo "rnoose." Older tags are very hard to find, and now that Chocolate has retired, they've become valuable very quickly! **TEENIE BEANIE (FIRST SET)**

Born 4/27/93 • Released 1/8/94 • Retired 12/31/98 • Estimated Value: ❶ $250
❷ $150 ❸ $75 ❹ $7 ❺ $7

CHOPS THE LAMB RECOMMENDED

Sweet little Chops was only out a year before her retirement in January 1997. The ivory-colored, black-faced lamb may have been retired because her name too closely matched that of Shari Lewis's puppet, Lamb Chop. It's almost certain that Chops's retirement was unplanned, because she was the only McDonald's Teenie Beanie "mom" already retired when the Teenies first came out in April 1997. The combination of her moderately early retirement and her status as a "mom" makes it quite likely that her value will increase significantly. Note the misspelling of the word "surely" in some of Chops's tags! **TEENIE BEANIE (FIRST SET)**

Born 5/3/96 • Released 1/7/96 • Retired 1/1/97 • Estimated Value: ❸ $175 ❹ $120

CLAUDE THE CRAB RECOMMENDED

Claude was presented to the world at the same time the previous crab, Digger (see page 28), was retired. Claude became popular immediately, though his tie-dyed colors are more muted than those of tie-dyes like Coral the fish (below), Garcia the bear (page 36), Flutter the butterfly (page 34), Peace the bear (page 58), and the new Neon the seahorse (page 54). Collectors who own an early Claude should check his hang tag to see if his name is spelled in all capital letters. This error appeared on only a few Beanies and makes them more valuable. **TEENIE BEANIE (THIRD SET)**

Born 9/3/96 • Released 5/11/97 • Retired 12/31/98 • Estimated Value: ❹ $7 ❺ $7

CONGO THE GORILLA

Like Bessie the cow, Congo's birthday is actually after his release date! But, unlike Bessie, Congo comes with a fourth-generation (or later) hang tag that originally had a birthday and a poem. The black and dark-brown Congo is a great addition to any Beanie collection, and collectors don't have to go bananas looking for him: Despite his December 1998 retirement, he's still available. Congo was used as a promotion at the 1998 Toy Fair in New York City.

Born 11/9/96 • Released 6/15/96 • Retired 12/31/98 • Estimated Value: ❹ $7 ❺ $7

CORAL THE FISH HIGHLY RECOMMENDED

The neat thing about Coral and the rest of the tie-dye Beanies is that each is unique. Because each has a different color and pattern, in an entire school of Corals, no two look the same. The tie-dye Beanies—whether current or retired—are very popular, but since Coral retired before the Teenie Beanies brought in a new school of collectors, she's in demand for that reason, too. The Coral pictured here has particularly vibrant colors.

Born 3/2/95 • Released 6/3/95 • Retired 1/1/97 • Estimated Value: ❸ $185 ❹ $125

CRUNCH THE SHARK

Because of potential conflicts with both a cereal name and the name of a chocolate bar, Crunch is another Beanie about whom rumors ran wild. Crunch appeared on "Top 10" retirement lists almost since his introduction in January 1997. He finally did retire in September 1998. Definitely more popular with boys than he is with girls, this shark, surprisingly realistic with steel-blue plush and plentiful white teeth, looks just about ready to swim off this page. Just when you thought it was safe to go back into the water...!

Born 1/13/96 • Released 1/1/97 • Retired 9/24/98 • Estimated Value: ❹ $7 ❺ $7

CUBBIE THE BEAR RECOMMENDED

One of the original nine Beanies, Cubbie was first released as "Brownie." The only difference between Brownie and Cubbie is the name tag; if there's not a first-generation hang tag that says Brownie, you're looking at Cubbie, so don't be fooled! A few fifth-generation Cubbies snuck out before Cubbie's retirement; this version will be worth a little more on the secondary market. Cubbie became the first professional sports-promotion Beanie when he was given away at a Chicago Cubs game on May 18, 1997.

Brownie: Born n/a • Released 1993 • Retired Prior to 1/8/94 • Estimated Value: ❶ $2,250
Cubbie: Born 11/14/93 • Released 1/8/94 • Retired 12/31/97 • Estimated Value: ❶ $250
❷ $150 ❸ $75 ❹ $15

CURLY THE BEAR RECOMMENDED

Curly was one of the first two Beanies with "napped" fur. As you can see, this napped fur is quite different from the usual smooth plush found on other Beanies. Scottie the Scottish Terrier (page 69), also with napped fur, was released at the same time as Curly—June 1996. Watch for an error on Curly's tag in which "surely" is spelled "surly" in the poem. Like some of the other Beanies with fifth-generation tags, the word "original" was spelled "origiinal" on his tag. Curly, who was always a favorite in the retirement rumor mill, shares a style number with the cranberry old- and new-faced Teddies (page 82).

Born 4/12/96 • Released 6/15/96 • Retired 12/31/98 • Estimated Value: ❹ $15 ❺ $12

DAISY THE COW RECOMMENDED

One of the few Beanies who survived all five generations of hang tags, Daisy was designed as a lay down–style cow, while her cow-nterpart, Bessie, was designed as a "sit-up" cow (see page 17). The white spot on Daisy's back is a mirror image of Spot the dog's black spot (see page 77). On very rare occasions, a spotless Daisy can be found as well. Daisy was only the second "special edition" Beanie with a specially printed second hang tag. This tag honors the late Chicago Cubs announcer Harry Caray with a poem and a caricature of Harry. This version was given out to fans at Wrigley Field on May 3, 1998.

Born 5/10/94 • Released 6/25/94 • Retired 9/15/98 • Estimated Value: ❶ $250 ❷ $175 ❸ $75 ❹ $9 ❺ $8

DERBY THE HORSE

Derby has been redesigned into four distinct Beanies. The first, limited-production version features a thin-yarn mane and tail and third-generation hang tags. The second version features thicker yarn on the mane and tail; the third has a white star on his forehead and has fifth-generation tags only. The most recent Derby has a fuzzy mane and tail similar to Roary the lion's mane (see page 66). The second and third versions are pictured at left.

Fine mane: Born 9/16/95 • Released 6/3/95 • Retired (unknown) • Estimated Value: ❸ $1,800 **Coarse mane:** Born 9/16/95 • Released (unknown) • Retired 12/15/97 • Estimated Value: ❸ $250 ❹ $17 ❺ $15 **With star:** Born 9/16/95 • Released 12/15/97 • Retired October '98 • Estimated Value: ❺ $7 **Fuzzy mane:** Born 9/16/95 • Released 12/15/97 • Retired 5/26/99 • Estimated Value: ❺ $7

DIGGER THE CRAB HIGHLY RECOMMENDED

Released with the second group of Beanies in mid-1994, the original Digger was bright orange, just like Chocolate the moose's antlers (see page 24). The orange Digger can be seen wearing the first three generations of hang tags. He was on the market about a year before he was redesigned into the better-known red Digger (third- and fourth-generation tags), pictured here. As retired Beanies go, red Digger is still a pretty good bargain. Now would be a good time to find one. Orange Digger is really quite stunning, but as an older retired, sadly, he's not as affordable.

Orange: Born 8/23/95 • Released 6/25/94 • Retired 6/3/95 • Estimated Value: ❶ $600 ❷ $500 ❸ $450 **Red:** Born 8/23/95 • Released 6/3/95 • Retired 5/11/97 • Estimated Value: ❸ $150 ❹ $80

DOBY THE DOBERMAN

O h, what excitement one little dog can bring! When McDonald's announced a second set of Teenie Beanies to be released in May 1998, trying to guess which Beanies would become Teenie Beanies became a top priority among collectors. And then the black-and-brown plush Teenie Doby appeared at a swap meet in his teenie bag with a large "No. 1" on it! The question of which Teenie would be first was answered, and the rush was on to pick up Doby in order to have matching "moms" and Teenie Babies. The grammatical error (its instead of it's) in Doby's poem has not affected his worth. TEENIE BEANIE (SECOND SET)

Born 10/9/96 • Released 1/1/97 • Retired 12/31/98 • Estimated Value: ❹ $7 ❺ $7

DOODLE THE ROOSTER HIGHLY RECOMMENDED

D oodle was a short-lived Beanie, due to a trademark conflict with a fast-food chain whose mascot is a rooster named—you guessed it—Doodles. The Beanie rumor mill predicted this conflict, and collectors rushed to purchase the yellow-and-pink tie-dyed Doodle while they could. Within just a couple months of his release, Doodle was renamed Strut (see page 80), but, unlike Tabasco/Snort (pages 81 and 73) and Sparky/Dotty (pages 74 and 30), Strut wasn't redesigned. Again, a short release time may prove to be a boon to collectors who were lucky enough to pick up Doodle before his retirement. They are predicting a significant increase in his value over time.

Born 3/8/96 • Released 5/11/97 • Retired 7/12/97 • Estimated Value: ❹ $30

DOTTY THE DALMATIAN

Dotty's arrival on the Beanie scene was noted early, with collectors "spotting" her tush tag on Sparky the Dalmatian. (Sparky was retired due to a trademark conflict with the National Fire Protection Association.) Dotty, who sports black ears and a black tail, can be distinguished at a distance from the retired Sparky, whose tail and ears are white (see page 74). In an odd reversal, Dotty has been found with Sparky tags! Not surprisingly, Dotty and Sparky share a style number.

Born 10/17/96 • Released 5/11/97 • Retired 12/31/98 • Estimated Value: ❹ $7 ❺ $7

EARLY THE ROBIN

Early was released with a whole flock of birds (six, to be exact) in the May 30, 1998, announcement. One of the least flashy of the avian Beanies, Early is notable for the bright red plush on his breast. As you can see from this photo, this red plush truly stands out! The brown tie-dyed plush covering the rest of his body is the same as that on Pounce the brown tie-dyed cat (see page 60).

Born 2/20/97 • Released 5/30/98 • Current • Estimated Value: ❺ $5–7

EARS THE BROWN RABBIT `RECOMMENDED`

The oldest of the Beanie Baby bunnies, Ears was made in the lay-down style. While the pastel Floppity, Hippity, and Hoppity (pages 34, 41, and 43, respectively) are stylized, Ears looks more realistic. His rich brown plush and long ears make him inviting. Some collectors have reported darker plush and a slightly larger head on fifth-generation versions, but it's likely this is just a difference in production runs. Ears was retired in May 1998.

Born 4/18/95 • Released 1/7/96 • Retired 5/1/98 • Estimated Value: ❸ $75 ❹ $15 ❺ $12

ECHO THE DOLPHIN RECOMMENDED

When first released to replace the retiring Flash the dolphin (page 33) and Splash the whale (page 76), Waves the new whale (page 87) and Echo caused a lot of confusion with an identity crisis of their own. The first productions of Echo and Waves had reversed hang and tush tags! Even though, as you can see from this photo, Echo clearly resembles a dolphin, it was months before word finally got around about the mix-up. Until then, Echo was called Waves by many collectors. Finally, the tags were switched and Echo gained her true identity. Now that Echo has retired, the mistagged version will gain strength on the secondary market. Given her moderately short life as a current, even correctly tagged Echoes should do well.

Born 12/21/96 • Released 5/11/97 • Retired 5/1/98 • Estimated Value: 💜 $15 💜 $12

EGGBERT THE HATCHING CHICK

Cute as a real baby chick, Eggbert is hatching from a smooth white plush eggshell. Eggbert himself has a bright yellow plush that's sculpted like the plush you see on Beak the kiwi bird (see page 17). As you can see, Eggbert's beak is a cone of bright orange plush, and he has embroidered black thread nostrils and big black eyes. Collectors wonder if Eggbert's name might prove problematic (a conflict with the old children's stories that feature Eggbert as a main character, maybe?), forcing an early retirement.

Born 4/10/98 • Released 1/1/99 • Current • Estimated Value: 💜 $5–7

ERIN THE BEAR ▓HIGHLY RECOMMENDED

The original "colored" bears were retired in early 1996, but Erin and Princess (page 61) seemed to foretell the next wave. Erin, like Princess, was introduced in an announcement separate from the release of a retirement or new set of Beanies, and she was a complete surprise to collectors. Her bright green color and embroidered white shamrock seen at left make her a standout in the Beanie crowd. Originally released in limited production, her price started out quite high. She was retired unexpectedly in May 1999, so buy her soon if you can. Protect yourself against counterfeits by buying only through a Ty retailer! **TEENIE INTERNATIONAL BEAR, BEANIE BUDDY**

Born 3/17/97 • Released 1/31/98 • Retired 5/21/99 • Estimated Value: ❺ $7

EUCALYPTUS THE KOALA

After retiring Mel the koala (page 52), Ty was quick to introduce a replacement. Eucalyptus is proof positive that you are what you eat (koalas are known to eat the leaves of eucalyptus trees). His gray plush is accented by his cream-colored belly, inner ears, and paw pads. Like many of the more recent Beanies, Eucalyptus also has embroidered toes.

Born 4/28/99 • Released 4/8/99 • Current • Estimated Value: ❺ $5–7

EWEY THE LAMB

The latest in the Beanie flock of sheep, Ewey, who was released in January 1999, is fashioned in Ty's newer long-legged body style. Ewey is nappy, like the earlier lamb, Fleece (see opposite page), but she is cream-colored rather than pure white like her predecessor. Ewey has a pink face with a pink plastic nose and pink embroidered nose and mouth. Ewey's mouth can be found either curved up in a smile or down in a frown. Neither is considered more valuable than the other at the moment.

Born 3/1/98 • Released 1/1/99 • Current • Estimated Value: ❺ $5–7

FETCH THE GOLDEN RETRIEVER `RECOMMENDED`

etch is one pip of a Beanie pup! Similar to Spunky the Cocker Spaniel (see page 77) in style, Fetch has a cousin in Ty's line of plush animals in Muffin (just like Wrinkles the Bulldog has in Winston and Churchill). As you can see in this photo, Fetch's fur is a light golden cream color, but what the picture doesn't tell you is how incredibly soft Fetch's coat is—just like the fur of a real Golden Retriever pup. Because Fetch was a current for such a short period of time, he will be especially prized.

Born 2/4/97 • Released 5/30/98 • Retired 12/31/98 • Estimated Value: ♥5 $7

FLASH THE DOLPHIN `HIGHLY RECOMMENDED`

lash and her pal, Splash the whale (featured on page 76), were the first two of the original nine Beanies to be retired. It is easy to confuse Flash with Manny the manatee (shown on page 51), who was retired at the same time. Collectors can tell them apart because Flash, shown here, has a white belly, while Manny's is gray. Flash reportedly has been spotted with two different tag poems.

Born 5/13/93 • Released 1/8/94 • Retired 5/11/97 • Estimated Value: ♥1 $300
♥2 $200   ♥3 $125   ♥4 $85

FLEECE THE LAMB

hen Chops the lamb was retired, Fleece took her place. Unlike Chops, who was ivory-colored with a black face (see page 24), Fleece is white as snow, as you can see here. Fleece was the third Beanie to feature "napped" fur rather than the usual plush. Though she's often thought of as an Easter Beanie (like the Beanie bunnies), she also fits right in with the rest of the farm Beanies. Fleece retired at the end of 1998.

Born 3/21/96 • Released 1/1/97 • Retired 12/31/98 • Estimated Value: ♥4 $7   ♥5 $7

FLIP THE WHITE CAT   HIGHLY RECOMMENDED

As with all the white Beanies, keeping Flip clean can be a problem—especially because it's hard to resist cuddling this little kitty. Flip shares her style number with another all-white Beanie, Chilly the polar bear (featured on page 23). Flip became very hard to find just before she was retired in October 1997. As a result, collectors paid a premium for her as a new retired. Since that time, her price has dropped a bit, making her a good choice for a future investment.

Born 2/28/95 • Released 1/7/96 • Retired 10/1/97 • Estimated Value: ❸ $75 ❹ $25

FLOPPITY THE LILAC BUNNY   RECOMMENDED

Floppity is the lilac-colored one-third of the pastel bunny trio that was released in January 1997. After their second Easter holiday as current Beanies, Floppity, Hippity (page 41), and Hoppity (page 43) were among the May 1998 retirees. If you have a fifth-generation Floppity, look in the yellow star on the front of the hang tag to see if "original" is spelled "origiinal," and check the back to see if "surface" is spelled "suface." Lucky collectors may even have one of the rare tags that has a sticker over "suface" to correct the misspelling!

Born 5/28/96 • Released 1/1/97 • Retired 5/1/98 • Estimated Value: ❹ $15 ❺ $12

FLUTTER THE BUTTERFLY   RECOMMENDED

Each Flutter is unique because of her rainbow tie-dyed plush. As this photo shows, only her little black eyes and black string antennae show the difference between her front and back. It's too bad Flutter was retired before poems were introduced, because her grace and beautiful tie-dyed plush certainly would have inspired a wonderful poem. Flutter is a highly desirable Beanie; unfortunately, her high price puts her out of range for many collectors.

Born n/a • Released 6/3/95 • Retired 6/15/96 • Estimated Value: ❸ $700

FORTUNE THE PANDA `RECOMMENDED`

Fortune's release in May 1998 brought good luck to Beanie collectors who had long waited for a replacement for the rare Peking (shown on page 59). Unlike Peking, Fortune is a sit up–style bear. He doesn't bear the "new face" found on other new bears like Peace, Princess, and Erin (pages 58, 61, and 32, respectively). This photo shows how very different Fortune is from these other bears: In contrast to the pouty nose accenting the face of those bears, Fortune's nose is pointed. The patches on his eyes aren't felt like Peking's either, but rather are made of black plush sewn into the pattern of his face.

Born 12/6/97 • Released 5/30/98 • Current • Estimated Value: ❤5 $5–7

FRECKLES THE LEOPARD

Some of the fourth-generation Freckles were shipped with a hang tag that erroneously listed his birthday as July 28, 1996, instead of his true birthday, June 3, 1996. The tag with the July birthday sometimes commands a small price premium among collectors who like "oddball"

Beanies. This freckled (what else?) feline with the cute pink nose is just as handsome as his picture suggests. Recently retired, Freckles should still be fairly easy to spot on the shelf of your local retailer. TEENIE BEANIE (THIRD SET)

Born 6/3/96 • Released 6/15/96 • Retired 12/31/98 • Estimated Value: ❤4 $7   ❤5 $7

Fuzz the Bear

Fuzz sure lives up to his name! Made from a new plush of trimmed chenille-like material, he is as soft as can be. His plush is the color of mustard, and he sports a navy blue ribbon around his neck, as shown here. Like all the new-faced bears, he has black eyes and an oval nose, which, on Fuzz's fuzzy mug, is black. Fuzz, who was the last of the January 1999 releases to appear in stores, is a great addition to all Beanie collections—not only because he is a member of the popular bear group, but also because he is a little different from all the other Beanies. BEANIE BUDDY

Born 7/23/98 • Released 1/1/99 • Current • Estimated Value: ❺ $5–7

Garcia the Bear   HIGHLY RECOMMENDED

Garcia, who shares a style number with the teal Teddies, was named for the late Jerry Garcia, lead singer for the popular band, Grateful Dead, and is right on the money with his rainbow tie-dye (see photo). Garcia's birthday takes the month and day from Jerry's own birthday, and the year from the year of his death. Garcia may have been retired due to conflicts stemming from the settling of the late singer's estate. There's a grammatical error in Garcia's poem (use instead of used), but this minor flaw has not affected his worth in any way. Garcia has been and remains one of the most popular Beanies.

Born 8/1/95 • Released 1/7/96 • Retired 5/11/97 • Estimated Value: ❸ $225 ❹ $140

GERMANIA THE BEAR

With the release of the exclusive Germania, Germany became the fourth country to be represented by a Beanie Babies bear. Germania, whose birthday is the date of the German reunification, is made of plush similar in color and texture to Fuzz the bear's (see photos, right and page 36). The black, red, and yellow German flag is embroidered on her chest, and she has thin red and yellow ribbons tied around her neck. She'll be hard to come by for U.S. collectors.

Born 10/3/90 • Released 1/1/99 • Current • Estimated Value: $10–12

GIGI THE POODLE

Lately it seems that with just about every new release, Ty includes at least one new Beanie that features nappy plush. Gigi the little black Poodle is a little bit different from the rest of the nappy-fur Beanies. Not only does Gigi have nappy black plush, she has smooth black plush as well! As you can see from this photo, the combination of nappy and smooth plush, complete with red bows on her ears, is what gives Gigi her Poodle-do. This stylized canine is a well-groomed standout among the Beanie dogs.

Born 3/7/97 • Released 5/30/98 • Current • Estimated Value: $5–7

GLORY THE BEAR   HIGHLY RECOMMENDED

Glory be, this bear is popular! But that shouldn't surprise anyone, with bears being the most popular Beanie group. This flag-bearing, red-and-blue spangled bear joined the group of patriotic Beanie Babies on May 30, 1998, and retired quickly. On July 7, 1998, Ty made the day of 50,000 fans at the Major League Baseball All-Star Game by handing out a Glory and a commemorative card to everyone attending the game. TEENIE INTERNATIONAL BEAR

Born 7/4/97 • Released 5/30/98 • Retired 12/31/98 • Estimated Value: $7

GOATEE THE MOUNTAIN GOAT

Goatee's plush is the same plush you'll see on the 1999 Signature Bear (see page 14)—a mixture of tan and gray threads. The insides of his ears and his horns are made from dark taupe felt, as you can see at right. He has a tan beard and tail made from the same material found on the new Derbys (page 28) and Mystics (page 54). Goatee's cute little beard makes it easy to see where he got his name. This is one goat you'll definitely want to get!

Born 11/4/98 • Released 1/1/99 • Current • Estimated Value: **5** $5–7

GOBBLES THE TURKEY `RECOMMENDED`

Gobbles started her life as the most difficult to find of the five holiday-release Beanie Babies from October 1997. After that, she became a bit more accessible. Pre-release pictures of this Thanksgiving Beanie didn't do her justice. When she finally showed up in stores, collectors loved fanning out her tail, as it is fanned out above, to show her in all her glory.

Born 11/27/96 • Released 10/1/97 • Retired 3/31/99 • Estimated Value: **4** $7   **5** $7

GOLDIE THE GOLDFISH `HIGHLY RECOMMENDED`

Goldie was the first of the Beanie fish trio to be released and the last to be retired. As you can see, her bright orange plush really makes her look like a goldfish! Despite Goldie's long reign as a current, she's been fairly difficult to find since her retirement—and her price has gone up accordingly. The matching Teenie Beanie counterpart also helps to drive up Goldie's price on the secondary market. TEENIE BEANIE (FIRST SET)

Born 11/14/94 • Released 6/25/94 • Retired 12/31/97 • Estimated Value: **1** $250
2 $150   **3** $75   **4** $25

GOOCHY THE JELLYFISH

One of the most unusual Beanie Babies to date, Goochy became a favorite among collectors. He quickly went through a change in plush; time will tell if it's permanent. Originally released with a shiny velour-like plush of pale pastel tie-dye, his colors were changed to slightly brighter pastels, but the shine remained. Goochy's oval eyes are embroidered on his large head, and, as you can see, he has 10 alternating short and long wiggly legs.

Pale: Born 11/18/98 • Released 1/1/99 • Retired March '99 (approximate) • Estimated Value: 💟 $8
Bright: Born 11/18/98 • Released March '99 (approximate) • Current • Estimated Value: 💟 $5–7

GRACIE THE SWAN   RECOMMENDED

Just as her poem implies, when Gracie was first released, collectors thought she was too plain. But she has since become more popular. This photo shows that Gracie is quite lovely. A September 13, 1998, promotion by Ty and the Chicago Cubs linked Gracie with Cubs' first baseman Mark Grace. Expect the promotional Gracie to be a home run on the secondary market, especially since she was retired prior to the game.

Born 6/17/96 • Released 1/1/97 • Retired 5/1/98 • Estimated Value: 💟 $10 💟 $8

GRUNT THE RAZORBACK   RECOMMENDED

Grunt found popularity among boys because of his rough-and-tough image. But Grunt also has a built-in following consisting of fans of the University of Arkansas Razorbacks! Collectors should check the felt spikes along his back and his white felt tusks for signs of wear. Try to find a Grunt that looks like the one at right. Grunt remains one of the more expensive of the May 1997 retirees. "Wrinkled" Grunts may be counterfeit.

Born 7/19/95 • Released 1/7/96 • Retired 5/11/97 • Estimated Value: 💟 $210 💟 $110

HALO THE ANGEL BEAR RECOMMENDED

This beautiful bear's white plush literally shimmers in the light. Her wings and halo are made from the same iridescent material as Magic the dragon's wings and spine (see page 51). Unlike the satin ribbons sported by the other bears, Halo's ribbon is sheer pink material with a thin gold edging on either side. Halo immediately became one of the most highly sought-after of the fall 1998 releases, perhaps due to her rare beauty, but perhaps because collectors believe she may be related to Princess, the royal purple Beanie bear issued in honor of Princess Diana. This speculation surfaced thanks to Halo's birthday, which happens to be the first anniversary of Diana's death. Many collectors have petitioned Ty to never retire Halo in order to preserve the memory of Diana.

Born 8/31/98 • Released 9/30/98 • Current • Estimated Value: 🖤 $5–7

HAPPY THE HIPPO HIGHLY RECOMMENDED

Originally released with gray plush, Happy was changed to this lavender color in mid-1995 (shown here). Ty may have thought that a gray hippo wasn't fanciful enough for children. With his long lifespan, Happy had lost favor for a while—until it was discovered that he was going to be released as part of the second McDonald's Teenie Beanie collection! Add to this his desirability as a May 1998 retiree, and Happy should be a good bet on the secondary market. TEENIE BEANIE (SECOND SET)

Gray: Born 2/25/94 • Released 6/25/94 • Retired 6/3/95 • Estimated Value: 🖤 $600 🖤 $500 🖤 $425 Lavender: Born 2/25/94 • Released 6/3/95 • Retired 5/1/98 • Estimated Value: 🖤 $175 🖤 $17 🖤 $15

HIPPIE THE TIE-DYE BUNNY

After the retirement of Floppity (page 34), Hippity (below), and Hoppity (page 43), Ty returned to the sit up–style bunny with the pastel tie-dye Hippie. Because of the tie-dyed fabric, every Hippie is unique, but the colors you'll see are mostly light pinks, yellows, blues, and greens, with touches of lavender, along with a white tail. The undersides of Hippie's lengthy ears are covered in a short pink plush, and he sports a pink triangle nose and pink whiskers. Unlike the first bunny trio, Hippie doesn't have a ribbon, so don't worry if it's missing on the Hippie you're looking at—there never was one!

Born 5/4/98 • Released 1/1/99 • Current • Estimated Value: $5–7

HIPPITY THE MINT BUNNY   RECOMMENDED

This "cool" mint bunny has long, floppy ears like his two pastel bunny buddies, Floppity and Hoppity (see pages 34 and 43). In the summer and early fall of 1997, Hippity was the most difficult of the trio to find. All the bunnies were in demand for the 1998 Easter holiday, amidst rumors they would be retired. Sure enough, they were retired shortly after Easter. The early-fifth-generation Hippitys have the same tag typos as Floppity, Hoppity, Blackie, Curly, Peace, and Valentino, with the double-i "origiinal" and missing-r "suface." More-recent Hippitys can be found with a sticker with the correct spelling covering the "suface" misspelling, so check those tags! BEANIE BUDDY

Born 6/1/96 • Released 1/1/97 • Retired 5/1/98 • Estimated Value: $15 $12

HISSY THE SNAKE RECOMMENDED

Hissy is a coveted Beanie for many collectors, who love his coiled shape. This long-awaited replacement for the retired Slither (page 71) isn't quite as long as his serpentine friend when he's stretched out, but he's long enough to be the second-longest Beanie. Hissy's back is a deep-blue tie-dyed plush similar to what is seen on Bronty the brontosaurus (see page 20), and his belly is a flashy bright yellow. As this photo shows, Hissy also has a bright-red felt tongue that may show signs of wear, so collectors should be careful when shopping the secondary market.

Born 4/4/97 • Released 12/31/97 • Retired 3/31/99 • Estimated Value: 🟋 $7

HOOT THE OWL HIGHLY RECOMMENDED

This tiny owl is one of the shortest Beanies made and can fit in even a small child's hand. Check out the poem on fourth-generation Hoots to see if the word "quite" is misspelled "qutie." Though not as rare as some other tag errors, this mistake does make Hoot more valuable. Since his retirement in October 1997, this retiree's value has started to climb, but Hoot is still inexpensive enough to add to almost any collection.

Born 8/9/95 • Released 1/7/96 • Retired 10/1/97 • Estimated Value: 🟋 $75 🟋 $25

HOPE THE PRAYING BEAR

Styled after a bear in Ty's plush line, the gold Hope is kneeling in prayer (see photo). Her paws and nose are cream-colored, and the toes on each paw are embroidered in black. Her nose is a soft patch of short chocolate plush. Hope has been released as one of Ty's Beanie Buddies, and it's possible we may end up seeing her white plush line sister, Faith, as a Beanie Baby in the future. **BEANIE BUDDY**

Born 3/23/98 • Released 1/1/99 • Current • Estimated Value: 🟋 $5–7

HOPPITY THE ROSE BUNNY

Possibly the most popular of the original three pastel bunnies, this little rose-colored bunny has been in great demand. Though Hippity was hard to find for a while in 1997, at the start of the 1998 Easter holiday Hoppity seemed to be the bunny in hiding. Since she hopped off into retirement, she has become harder to find. She's well worth the investment, however, since she's likely to become more scarce over time. As on the other pastel bunnies, the fifth-generation tag misspells the word "original" as "origiinal," and "surface" is spelled without the "r" on the back. Lucky collectors might find one of the rare Hoppitys with the sticker that corrects the "suface" error.

Born 4/3/96 • Released 1/1/97 • Retired 5/1/98 • Estimated Value: ♥ $15 ♥ $12

HUMPHREY THE CAMEL

Who could resist this dromedary who can't even stand on his own four legs (see photo)? Humphrey's forlorn expression and floppy legs make him a prized member of any Beanie collection. Humphrey was retired early in Beanie history and is difficult to find in mint condition with his tag. His retired pricing reflects it, but there are still many people who long to have a Beanie classic like Humphrey—with or without his hang tag. BEANIE BUDDY

Born n/a • Released 6/25/94 • Retired 6/15/95 • Estimated Value: ♥ $1,800 ♥ $1,650 ♥ $1,500

IGGY THE IGUANA RECOMMENDED

The first shipments of Iggy and Rainbow the chameleon seemed to have switched tags, but it was actually their fabric that was switched (see photo). A felt tongue was added to the rainbow Iggy before his fabric was corrected to blue tie-dye. TEENIE BEANIE (THIRD SET)

Rainbow plush, no tongue: Born 8/12/97 • Released 12/31/97 • Retired mid-May '98 • Estimated Value: 🖤5 $10 Rainbow plush, with tongue: Born 8/12/97 • Released mid-May '98 • Retired mid-September '98 • Estimated Value: 🖤5 $12 Blue plush: Born 8/12/97 • Released mid-August '98 • Retired 3/31/99 • Estimated Value: 🖤5 $7

INCH THE INCHWORM HIGHLY RECOMMENDED

Rainbow-colored segments and a wavy body make Inch look as if he actually wiggles his way along. Inch was originally introduced with felt antennae instead of the newer yarn, but the felt didn't wear well (just like Lizzy's and Slither's tongues). Both versions are shown here. TEENIE BEANIE (SECOND SET)

Felt antennae: Born 9/3/95 • Released 6/3/95 • Retired 10/15/96 • Estimated Value: 🖤3 $170 🖤4 $140 Yarn antennae: Born 9/3/95 • Released 10/15/96 • Retired 5/1/98 • Estimated Value: 🖤4 $18 🖤5 $15

INKY THE OCTOPUS HIGHLY RECOMMENDED

Inky was originally released in a tan color with no mouth (perhaps because an octopus's mouth is under his head). After three months, Ty added a V-shaped mouth; then, nine months after that, made him the pink color seen here. Another oddity is that Inky can be found with seven or nine legs instead of the usual eight.

Tan, no mouth: Born 11/29/94 • Released 6/25/94 • Retired 9/12/94 • Estimated Value: 🖤1 $600 🖤2 $500 Tan, with mouth: Born 11/29/94 • Released 9/12/94 • Retired 6/3/95 • Estimated Value: 🖤2 $550 🖤3 $450 Pink: Born 11/29/94 • Released 6/3/95 • Retired 5/1/98 • Estimated Value: 🖤3 $200 🖤4 $18 🖤5 $15

JABBER THE PARROT

Much quieter than a real parrot, the ever-colorful Jabber was an immediate hit with Beanie collectors when he flew onto the Beanie scene on May 30, 1998. It would be hard to find a Beanie with more different colors of plush. Only the multicolored Inch the inchworm comes close (see opposite page), but if the black-and-white striped plush around Jabber's eyes counts as two different colors, you'll notice that even Inch can't win. If you can cage this rare bird, you'll be one happy Beanie collector! **BEANIE BUDDY**

Born 10/10/97 • Released 5/30/98 • Current • Estimated Value: ❺ $5–7

JAKE THE MALLARD DUCK

This little duck will really quack you up! The second Beanie duck released (Quackers, page 63, was the first), Jake is very realistic looking, with a dark teal head and a white ring around his neck. You may need to do some hunting to bag this one, but beware of fakes! Amazingly, they appeared on the scene almost at the same time as the real thing. The head on at least one style of the fake Jakes is more green than the teal on the real deal. See the photo above to make note of the real color. **BEANIE BUDDY**

Born 4/16/97 • Released 5/30/98 • Current • Estimated Value: ❺ $5–7

JOLLY THE WALRUS   RECOMMENDED

Jolly was a welcome replacement for Tusk the walrus (page 85), who was retired in January 1997. Some collectors had considered Tusk boring. Though Jolly shared the same basic body shape with Echo the dolphin (page 31) and Waves the whale (page 87), his wonderful mustache won him immediate favor. As you can see, the long, soft fuzz makes Jolly unusual, which might be why he was tough to find in stores before his retirement. Collectors may have to do some serious hunting to locate him. Values should be strong based on his rather short stint as a current.

Born 12/2/96 • Released 5/11/97 • Retired 5/1/98 • Estimated Value: ❹ $12 ❺ $10

KICKS THE SOCCER BEAR

At a glance, Kicks looks to be bright green, but if you look closer, you'll see that this little new-faced bear really has both green and blue threads mixed into his plush. On his chest is a soccer ball embroidered in black and white thread. He's ribbonless, but that's okay, since a ribbon would probably get in the way of his playing soccer anyway! Kicks is likely to be extremely popular with anyone who is a fan of the game.

Born 8/16/98 • Released 1/1/99 • Current • Estimated Value: 💲 $5–7

KIWI THE TOUCAN RECOMMENDED

Kiwi is one confused Beanie! Kiwi fruit and kiwi birds are both indigenous to New Zealand; but toucans are native to Central and South America. This Beanie bird was released at the same time as his body double, Caw the crow (page 22), and was retired in January 1997. Since then, Kiwi's colorful beak (the same royal blue color as the rare version of Peanut the elephant, featured on page 58) and tail have gained great popularity. Check all third-generation Kiwi hang tags for his name in all lowercase letters; this variation might make him a little more valuable.

Born 9/16/95 • Released 6/3/95 • Retired 1/1/97 • Estimated Value: 💲 $175 💲 $115

KNUCKLES THE PIG

Collectors who missed out on Beanie original Squealer (page 77) will squeal instead over the new Beanie pig in the poke. In contrast to Squealer's bright pink plush, Knuckles is more subtle in color, as you can see from this picture—with the exception of his bright blue ribbon. (This little porker must have won first place at the State Fair!) His snout and paws are tan plush, and he has black thread nostrils.

Born 3/25/99 • Released 4/14/99 • Current • Estimated Value: 💲 $5–7

KUKU THE COCKATOO

Collectors will go cuckoo over this cockatoo with a fluff of pink feathery plush topping his head. Primarily white except for his gray beak and feet and the pretty pink plush under his wings, Kuku will require some special care to keep him clean and neat. Released with five other birds on May 30, 1998, Kuku is a great addition to any Beanie collection.

Born 1/5/97 • Released 5/30/98 • Current • Estimated Value: 🖤 $5–7

LEFTY THE DONKEY   HIGHLY RECOMMENDED

Patriotic Beanies Lefty, Righty the elephant (page 65), and Libearty the bear (page 48) were among the first to be released with a fourth-generation hang tag, some of which have "surface" spelled "sufrace" on the backs. All three Beanies were retired within six months of their announcements, making them some of the shortest-lived Beanies and the most valuable of the January 1997 retirees. Lefty and his Republican counterpart were released to commemorate the 1996 presidential election. As with all the patriotic Beanies, it's possible to find this little donkey without a flag or with an upside-down flag, two rare errors that greatly increase Lefty's value. The Lefty pictured here features the flag as it is supposed to be.

Born 7/4/96 • Released 6/15/96 • Retired 1/1/97 • Estimated Value: 🖤 $200

LEGS THE FROG

It's not easy being green. Poor little Legs was much maligned for being too plain (see photo), but as one of the original nine Beanies, he will always have a place in Beanie history. Even though he was retired relatively early (October 1997), Legs had been around long enough for most collectors to pick him up. This kept his price low, however, and his value has nowhere to go but up. You can still pick up this original at a very reasonable price, and that might be a pretty smart move.

Born 4/25/93 • Released 1/8/94 • Retired 10/1/97 • Estimated Value: ❤ $250 ❤ $150 ❤ $65 ❤ $15

LIBEARTY THE BEAR

Released to honor the 1996 Summer Olympics in Atlanta, Libearty had to relinquish the word "Olympics" from her tag because the International Olympic Committee would not give Ty permission to use it. Despite some people believing that the error is rare, Libeartys that have the word "Beanie" spelled "Beanine" are actually more common and slightly less valuable than correct Libeartys. Clear tag connectors and whited-out or cut-off Web site information are also common. Libearty, with her patriotic red and blue ribbons, has been the most popular of the American Beanies and has increased in value even more quickly than the two earliest members, Lefty the donkey (page 47) and Righty the elephant (page 65).

Born Summer '96 • Released 6/15/96 • Retired 1/1/97 • Estimated Value: ❤ $250

LIZZY THE LIZARD HIGHLY RECOMMENDED

Once Legs the frog (opposite page) was retired, it was clear from her poem that Lizzy wouldn't be far behind. Technically, Lizzy retired before fifth-generation hang tags came out, but she can be found sporting one. The original Lizzy featured tie-dyed plush, but she was redesigned with the black-and-blue plush and yellow belly pictured here. The redesigned Lizzy was one of the original McDonald's Teenie Beanies, although the Teenie version is named Lizz. Lizzy also can be found with an alternate version of her poem. **TEENIE BEANIE (FIRST SET)**

Tie-dyed: Born 5/11/95 • Released 6/3/95 • Retired 1/7/96 • Estimated Value: 3 $650 Blue: Born 5/11/95 • Released 1/7/96 • Retired 12/31/97 • Estimated Value: 3 $275 4 $15

LOOSY THE GOOSE

Flying into the Beanie Babies collection all the way from Canada, Loosy is a Canadian goose decked out in her finest—a maroon satin ribbon around her neck (see photo). Loosy's design is very close to that of Jake the mallard duck (pictured on page 45), but Loosy's neck is longer. With her black head and neck and her white plush "chin strap" and chest, she's realistic enough that collectors might almost expect to hear her honk!

Born 3/29/98 • Released 9/30/98 • Current • Estimated Value: 5 $5–7

LUCKY THE LADYBUG `HIGHLY RECOMMENDED`

Lucky first came out with seven felt spots glued onto her back, but, after almost two years, Ty switched to a fabric with printed spots. Many of the seven-spot Luckys have lost a little something as their glued-on spots have fallen off. The rarest of the variations is the 21-spot Lucky, whose spots were printed in the fabric, but you're most likely to find the 11-spot version seen here.

7 felt spots: Born 5/1/95 • Released 6/25/94 • Retired 2/27/96 • Estimated Value: ♥ $300 ♥ $225 ♥ $150 21 printed spots: Born 5/1/95 • Released 6/15/96 • Retired (unknown) • Estimated Value: ♥ $275 11 printed spots: Born 5/1/95 • Released 9/15/96 (approximate) • Retired 5/1/98 • Estimated Value: ♥ $17 ♥ $15

LUKE THE BLACK LAB

The minute you see him, you'll want to retrieve this little black Labrador from the store shelf. Luke is made from shiny black plush and features floppy ears with the long floppy-leg style of the newer Beanie Babies. You'll love the sweet expression on his face. Given the extreme popularity of Labs as pets, it's a good bet that Luke will earn widespread approval.

Born 6/15/98 • Released 1/1/99 • Current • Estimated Value: ♥ $5–7

MAC THE CARDINAL

Ty released Mac the cardinal in honor of Major League Baseball's St. Louis Cardinal Mark McGwire and his 1998 record-setting season. This little bright-red bird is topped off with a hairdo of red fur made of the same material as Roary the lion's mane (see page 66). Mac's beak and big, brown-rimmed eyes are set off with black plush, and his feet are black as well. Collectors will set their own records running home with Mac!

Born 6/10/98 • Released 1/1/99 • Current • Estimated Value: ♥ $5–7

MAGIC THE DRAGON HIGHLY RECOMMENDED

The only certain thing about Magic's variations is that there's nothing certain about them! The oldest versions have pale pink thread used in the stitching of her wings and nostrils, while slightly later versions use hot pink thread, as seen in this photo. The latest version can be found with both colors, and nobody seems to know which is more common. Also, the third-generation Magics usually have puffier wings than other versions. Pick up this magical white dragon with the beautiful iridescent wings before her price takes wing!

Born 6/8/95 • Released 6/3/95 • Retired 12/31/97 • Estimated Value: ❸ $85 ❹ $35

MANNY THE MANATEE RECOMMENDED

The all-gray Manny is often confused with the white-bellied Flash the dolphin (see page 33), especially since they were retired at the same time. But Manny was not as popular as Flash was as a current, nor was she available for as long as Flash was. As a result of her endangerment, her retired price has gone up faster than Flash's price. To clarify what Manny truly looks like, see the picture at left. A mint-condition Manny is still a good investment, especially if she sports a rare third-generation hang tag. A grammatical error in Manny's tag (like instead of likes) doesn't affect this Beanie's value.

Born 6/8/95 • Released 1/7/96 • Retired 5/11/97 • Estimated Value: ❸ $200 ❹ $125

MAPLE THE BEAR   HIGHLY RECOMMENDED

Released to commemorate Canadian Independence Day and available for retail sale only in Canada, Maple's original name was Pride. About 3,000 to 5,000 Beanie Babies were produced and released with a Pride tush tag. This original version is almost impossible to find, and the current Maple isn't much easier to find, even in Canada. A special version of this snow-white, red-beribboned bear was made available in limited edition during the last week of August 1997 to help benefit the Special Olympics. Being Canadian, all Maples have a second tush tag in both French and English. Buy carefully! There are counterfeits around. **TEENIE INTERNATIONAL BEAR**

Born 7/1/96 • Released 1/1/97 • Current • Estimated Value: ❹ $7 ❺ $5–7

MEL THE KOALA

When is a bear not really a bear? When it's a koala! Mel, like his Australian pals Pouch the kangaroo (page 60) and Eucalyptus (page 32), is really a marsupial. There were lots of rumors about Mel being retired because of the reference in his tag poem to actor "hunk" Mel Gibson, but after two years of Beaniehood, it became apparent that Mel was safe from trademark woes. He was retired in his own sweet time. It's likely that Teenie Mel, in the second set of McDonald's Teenie Beanies, will mean added value for Mel in his retirement years. **TEENIE BEANIE (SECOND SET)**

Born 1/15/96 • Released 1/1/97 • Retired 3/31/99 • Estimated Value: ❹ $7 ❺ $7

MILLENNIUM THE BEAR

This bright magenta new-faced bear will help collectors ring in the new millennium in fine fashion. His chest bears an embroidered Earth with a golden Sun on the horizon with the year "2000" underneath, as pictured at right. Millennium's ribbon is a copper-colored metallic edged in gold. Collectors take note—you may find his name spelled with only one "n" on the original version. This version will probably be slightly more valuable in the future, but there is no significant difference right now. **BEANIE BUDDY**

Born 1/1/99 • Released 1/1/99 • Current • Estimated Value: $5–7

MOOCH THE SPIDER MONKEY

Long, dangly arms and legs make Mooch a big hit. His body of black plush is offset by the longer white fuzzy fur around his face, while his hands, feet, ears, and face are made from a light tan plush (see photo). As befits an impish little monkey, Mooch's dark brown-rimmed eyes are larger than you'll see on most of the other Beanie Babies. As shown at left, his long tail has a kink at the end just like the kink in Bongo the monkey's tail (see page 19). Don't waste time monkeying around—make sure you add this cute little guy to your collection!

Born 8/1/98 • Released 1/1/99 • Current • Estimated Value: $5–7

MYSTIC THE UNICORN `HIGHLY RECOMMENDED`

Mystic's mane and tail were originally made of thin white yarn. The fine yarn gave way to coarser yarn. Rumors of a Mystic with a horn of the same material as Magic the dragon's wings abounded (see page 51) before two such Mystics were found in stores in summer 1997. Those Beanies were a prototype for the iridescent-horned Mystic that was released in October 1997. The last version (not pictured) sported a fuzzy mane and tail striped in pastel blue, pink, and yellow.

Fine mane: Born 5/21/94 • Released 6/25/94 • Retired (unknown) • Estimated Value: ❶ $375 ❷ $275 ❸ $200 Coarse mane: Born 5/21/94 • Released (unknown) • Retired 10/23/97 • Estimated Value: ❸ $100 ❹ $20 Iridescent horn: Born 5/21/94 • Released 10/23/97 • Retired October '98 • Estimated Value: ❹ $7 ❺ $7 Rainbow mane: Born 5/21/94 • Released October '98 • Retired 5/18/99 • Estimated Value: ❺ $7

NANOOK THE HUSKY `RECOMMENDED`

Collectors take one look at Nanook's big blue eyes and become hooked, and you can see why from his photo! His gray back and head are accented with bright white plush. This little Husky's popularity as a current should carry on now that he's retired. Nanook is a good buy on the secondary market. TEENIE BEANIE (THIRD SET)

Born 11/21/96 • Released 5/11/97 • Retired 3/31/99 • Estimated Value: ❹ $7 ❺ $7

NEON THE SEAHORSE

This Beanie's name will go up in lights, no doubt! Made from the popular tie-dye plush, Neon has two little horns on the top of his head and small wings on his back. As you can see, his tail is long and curled. The very first seahorse in the Beanie Babies collection—with a very cool design, as well—Neon is sure to go over swimmingly with collectors!

Born 4/1/99 • Released 4/8/99 • Current • Estimated Value: ❺ $5–7

NIBBLER THE RABBIT

Twin bunnies Nibbler and Nibbly were released at the same time as Hippie the tie-dye bunny (see page 41) in January 1999. These twin bunnies are more similar to Ears the brown rabbit (page 30) than they are to the sit up–style bunnies Floppity, Hippity, and Hoppity (pages 34, 41, and 43). Nibbler is off-white with a cream-colored fuzzy tail and tall ears. The inside of her ears, her nose, her whiskers, and her mouth are all pink. Nibbler will be popular as an Easter bunny, assuming, of course, that she's not retired before next Easter.

Born 4/6/98 • Released 1/1/99 • Current • Estimated Value: ❺ $5–7

NIBBLY THE RABBIT

Nibbly was released at the same time as Nibbler the rabbit, but these "twins" are not identical! Nibbly has the same plush as Scat the cat (see page 68): It's a mix of tan and greenish-gray, but, from a distance, Nibbly just looks brown. He's got the same pink nose, mouth, and whiskers as Nibbler. Since Nibbly has the same plush as Scat, many collectors think they'll be retired at the same time.

Born 5/7/98 • Released 1/1/99 • Current • Estimated Value: ❺ $5–7

NIP THE GOLD CAT   HIGHLY RECOMMENDED

The first version of Nip had a big, rounded head, white muzzle, white belly, and pink ears and whiskers. The second version (the rarest) was all gold with pink ears. The last, and most widely available, Nip (pictured here) had white ears, paws, and whiskers. She was retired before fifth-generation tags, but a few collectors have found a fifth-generation Nip.

White face and belly: Born 3/6/94 • Released 1/7/95 • Retired 1/7/96 • Estimated Value: ❷ $375
❸ $350 All gold: Born 3/6/94 • Released 1/7/96 • Retired 3/10/96 • Estimated Value: ❸ $700
White paws: Born 3/6/94 • Released 3/10/96 • Retired 12/31/97 • Estimated Value: ❸ $250 ❹ $15

NUTS THE SQUIRREL

As you can see, Nuts has the coolest tail of any of the Beanies: soft, full, and fluffy. This appealing characteristic, and the fact that Nuts is the only Beanie squirrel Ty has issued, should lend him extra value on the secondary market. He remained a current for two years, but now that he's retired—and a part of the third Teenie Beanie set—he will be worth having in your collection. **TEENIE BEANIE (THIRD SET)**

Born 1/21/96 • Released 1/1/97 • Retired 12/31/98 • Estimated Value: ♥ $7 ♥ $7

OSITO THE MEXICAN BEAR

Ty added a fifth country to its international bears with the release of Osito, whose name means "little bear" in Spanish. Like the other international bears, Osito brandishes his country's flag on his chest—this one is the green, white, and red colors of Mexico. This bear's plush is red, and in keeping with the Mexican color scheme, Osito sports green and white ribbons tied in a bow around his neck. Like the other international bears, Osito is being released only in his native country, so he will be difficult for U.S. collectors to come by.

Born 2/5/99 • Released 4/17/99 • Current • Estimated Value: ♥ $5–7

PATTI THE PLATYPUS HIGHLY RECOMMENDED

Patti is one of the original nine Beanies, but she underwent several color changes. Officially Patti has had only two colors, but it could be considered four. The first Patti, released before the original nine Beanies, is a deep fuchsia color with first-generation hang tag and black-and-white tush tag. The second and third versions are called raspberry and magenta, and the last version (shown at left) is a lighter fuchsia. To see what version yours is, hold her up next to Inch the inchworm's tail (see page 44). The last version matches Inch exactly. Patti was featured in the first set of McDonald's Teenie Beanies. TEENIE BEANIE (FIRST SET), BEANIE BUDDY

Raspberry, magenta, and deep fuchsia: Born 1/6/93 • Released 1/8/94 • Retired 2/28/95 • Estimated Value: ❶ $700 ❷ $600 ❸ $500 **Fuchsia:** Born 1/6/93 • Released 2/28/95 • Retired 5/1/98 • Estimated Value: ❸ $175 ❹ $18 ❺ $12

PAUL THE WALRUS

Eggbert is the Beanie eggman, but Paul is definitely the walrus! He's a cross between the first two Beanie walruses, Tusk and Jolly (pages 85 and 45, respectively). Paul's dark tan plush body is similar to Tusk's, but he has Jolly's mustache (and then some!) and white plush tusks. Collectors are anxiously waiting to see if John and George will join Paul and Ringo in the Beanie Babies collection!

Born 2/23/99 • Released 4/12/99 • Current • Estimated Value: ❺ $5–7

PEACE THE BEAR HIGHLY RECOMMENDED

Still unbelievably popular two years after his official release, tie-dyed Peace is one of the hardest current Beanies to find in stores due to his being the last of the May 1997 newbeans to be shipped. Decked out just like Garcia the bear, Peace sports a multicolored peace symbol embroidered on his chest. Pastel versions (like the one pictured at left) have been more sought after than those with brightly colored tie-dye patterns. Fifth-generation Peace has been shipped with the "origiinal" and "suface" misspellings on his tag. Peace only comes with the new Teddy face.

Born 2/1/96 • Released 5/11/97 • Current • Estimated Value: 4 $7 5 $5–7

PEANUT THE ELEPHANT HIGHLY RECOMMENDED

The royal blue Peanut is, without a doubt, the most sought-after Beanie. Released only for a very short period, and mainly before Beanie Babies became a national passion, Peanut's value has skyrocketed. The beautiful deep blue plush apparently was an error and was replaced with the more common light blue color. (Both are shown at right.) Peanut can also be seen as part of the second McDonald's Teenie Beanie set and will find new popularity since her retirement as collectors search for "moms" for their Teenies.

TEENIE BEANIE (SECOND SET), BEANIE BUDDY

Royal blue: Born 1/25/95 • Released 6/3/95 • Retired 10/2/95 • Estimated Value: 3 $3,750 Light blue: Born 1/25/95 • Released 10/2/95 • Retired 5/1/98 • Estimated Value: 3 $800 4 $17 5 $15

PECAN THE BEAR

Pecan, like Almond in the April 1999 releases, sports the "floppy" bear body style. This, along with the old face, new face, and lay-down styles, is the fourth Beanie bear body style. Though Ty has labeled Pecan a "gold" bear, he appears to be, well, pecan-colored. The bottoms of his paws are dark tan, and his toes, like many of the January and April 1999 releases, are embroidered into his paws. A member of the much-loved bear family, Pecan will be a great investment.

Born 4/15/99 • Released 4/8/99 • Current • Estimated Value: ⑤ $5–7

PEKING THE PANDA RECOMMENDED

Peking is one of the lay down–style bears released into the Beanie Babies collection. As you can see, the black felt circles around his eyes give him a sad air. Because he was retired before Beanies became hot, Peking is very difficult to find in mint condition, and almost impossible to find with his tags in any condition. Be wary of counterfeit Pekings that have come into the secondary market. Study him closely before you spend a lot of money to obtain this extremely rare specimen. BEANIE BUDDY

Born n/a • Released 6/25/94 • Retired 1/7/96 • Estimated Value: ❶ $1,600 ❷ $1,400 ❸ $1,200

PINCHERS THE LOBSTER RECOMMENDED

Pinchers, a member of the original nine Beanie Babies, was retired on May 1, 1998. Slightly redesigned from an early "Punchers" Beanie, this Pinchers's feelers were shortened slightly, and the inner two segments on his tail are closer together (see photo). Unless you see a hang tag that reads "Punchers," this Beanie is probably just an old Pinchers. Due to his Teenie counterpart from the second McDonald's promotion and his retired status, Pinchers remains a good investment. TEENIE BEANIE (SECOND SET)

Punchers: Born n/a • Released 1/8/94 • Retired (unknown) • Estimated Value: ❶ $2,500
Pinchers: Born 6/19/93 • Released 1/8/94 • Retired 5/1/98 • Estimated Value: ❶ $250
❷ $150 ❸ $75 ❹ $15 ❺ $12

PINKY THE FLAMINGO

Even non-collectors recognize long-legged Pinky. As you can see, her bright pink color, bright orange beak, and long legs distinguish her from the crowd—any crowd. Pinky has been difficult to find in some areas, thanks to her popularity as both a Beanie Buddy and a "mom" to the hardest-to-find Teenie Beanie from the original McDonald's set. She's going to be one hot flamingo now that she's retired. TEENIE BEANIE (FIRST SET), BEANIE BUDDY

Born 2/13/95 • Released 6/3/95 • Retired 12/31/98 • Estimated Value: ❸ $75 ❹ $8 ❺ $8

POUCH THE KANGAROO

Longtime rumors of Pouch's retirement were greatly exaggerated. Concerns about her little joey's head (see photo) coming unsewn from her pouch seem to be unfounded, but the rumors continued. During her time as a current, she became more difficult to find just before any Ty announcement—probably for that very reason. But Pouch is one cute kangaroo and a great addition to any collection—especially now that Ty has finally retired her.

Born 11/6/96 • Released 1/1/97 • Retired 3/31/99 • Estimated Value: ❹ $9 ❺ $7

POUNCE THE CAT RECOMMENDED

As this photo proves, this cute kitty really does have all-brown tie-dyed plush. It's not a mistake, even though many thought it might have been. The tie-dyed plush makes each Pounce unique. After Pounce's initial announcement, it didn't take long for people to start wondering if the name "Pounce" might cause yet another trademark problem, this time with a cat food by the same name. Given Pounce's short lifespan as a current, who knows if these musings held any truth?

Born 8/28/97 • Released 12/31/97 • Retired 3/31/99 • Estimated Value: ❺ $7

PRANCE THE CAT RECOMMENDED

The tiger stripes on Prance make her a stand-out from all the other Beanie cats. What a great addition to the cat collection she was! However, her stripes can cause manufacturing errors such as the stripes on one side being the wrong direction or her tail going the wrong way. She was only on the market for a short period of time, so she might be hard to find. Pick her up if you see her!

Born 11/20/97 • Released 12/31/97 • Retired 3/31/99 • Estimated Value: ♥5 $7

PRICKLES THE HEDGEHOG

Like Roam the buffalo (page 66) and Gigi the poodle (page 37), Prickles is a "combo" Beanie, featuring nappy brown plush on his back and smooth tan plush on his belly, face, and legs. His ears, like Tank the armadillo's, are made from felt. Prickles's long, pointy snout is tipped with a round plastic nose and black thread whiskers. Collectors immediately took a liking to this unusual Beanie, who is as cute as can be.

Born 2/19/98 • Released 1/1/99 • Current • Estimated Value: ♥5 $5–7

PRINCESS THE BEAR HIGHLY RECOMMENDED

Beautiful in every way, the deep royal purple Princess stole the hearts of collectors immediately. She is also highly desired by collectors of Princess Diana memorabilia. Ty announces on her unique hang tag that all profits will be donated to Diana's memorial fund. Many retailers followed Ty's lead and raffled or auctioned off Princess to raise money for various charities. Don't worry about whether Princess's tush tag says PVC or PE pellets: Even some of the first shipments contained the new PE pellets. Just be happy if you have this English Rose in your collection. BEANIE BUDDY

Born n/a • Released 10/29/97 • Retired 4/13/99 • Estimated Value: ♥4 $20 ♥5 $15

PUFFER THE PUFFIN HIGHLY RECOMMENDED

Reminiscent of the retired Kiwi the toucan (pictured on page 46), Puffer features a flashy red-and-yellow beak that made her a bright standout in the Beanie class of January 1998 (see photo). It was a big surprise to everyone when she flew off into retirement so quickly during the September 1998 announcements. Due to her short length of time on the market, expect her value to rise perhaps a bit faster than that of other retireds.

Born 11/3/97 • Released 12/31/97 • Retired 9/18/98 • Estimated Value: 5 $9

PUGSLY THE PUG

Pugsly the Pug dog is notable for his black snout and ears, his curly little tail, and his wrinkles. As a member of the popular Beanie dog family, Pugsly immediately became a valued member of any Beanie Baby collection. After almost two years as a current, this cute little Pug retired, so pick him up quickly, before he hits the secondary market and his price rises accordingly, if you haven't already done so.

Born 5/2/96 • Released 5/11/97 • Retired 3/31/99 • Estimated Value: 4 $7 5 $7

PUMKIN' THE PUMPKIN HIGHLY RECOMMENDED

His plush is as bright orange as any good jack o' lantern could hope for, but Pumkin' has long, gangly arms and legs of bright green. His face is crafted in black, with a great big happy grin, and he's capped off with a leafy topknot of green plush. Pumkin', a great addition to anyone's holiday decorations, was released just in time for the 1998 Halloween season, but collectors had to scramble to find him before the witching hour. He was retired shortly thereafter, on December 31, 1998.

Born 10/31/98 • Released 9/30/98 • Retired 12/31/98 • Estimated Value: 5 $18

QUACKERS THE DUCK `HIGHLY RECOMMENDED`

The very earliest examples of this bright yellow duck were shipped without wings. This wingless version is very rare and highly desirable, and almost impossible to find with his tag. Interestingly, some of the second-generation tags on both the wingless and winged versions record his name as "Quacker." Quackers's Teenie Beanie counterpart from the first McDonald's set is named Quacks. Quackers was retired on May 1, 1998.

TEENIE BEANIE (FIRST SET), BEANIE BUDDY

Wingless: Born 4/19/94 • Released 6/25/94 • Retired 1/7/95 • Estimated Value: ❶ $1,800 ❷ $1,600 **With wings:** Born 4/19/94 • Released 1/7/95 • Retired 5/1/98 • Estimated Value: ❷ $600 ❸ $75 ❹ $12 ❺ $10

RADAR THE BAT `RECOMMENDED`

Confusion reigned when Ty announced the retirement of both Radar and Spooky the ghost on January 29, 1997, then retracted the announcement the next day. Radar hung around until his retirement that May; Spooky (page 76) lasted until December 31, 1997. Radar doesn't have the Velcro hook-and-loop fasteners on his wings that his replacement Batty has (see page 16), but he folds up very neatly when his wings are wrapped around his body. As you can see in this photo, Radar has bright red eyes that belie the fact that bats don't see very well; bats do most of their navigating by a type of—what else?—radar!

Born 10/30/95 • Released 9/1/95 • Retired 5/11/97 • Estimated Value: ❸ $175 ❹ $120

RAINBOW THE CHAMELEON RECOMMENDED

Confusion reigned with the release of Rainbow and Iggy the iguana (see page 44). Originally thought to be a double mistag, time has shown collectors that the two were actually reptiles of a different color. Rainbow, with his plush "collar," was released with Iggy's blue tie-dyed fabric (shown below) rather than with the rainbow colors mentioned in his name and his poem. After Iggy went through an intermediate step, in which he gained a felt tongue, the two began shipping correctly. Rainbow has regained his bright tie-dyed fabric as well as his tongue (also shown here). The blue plush version will likely end up as the more valuable of the two Rainbows.

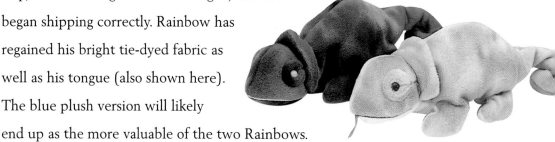

Blue tie-dye plush: Born 10/14/97 • Released 12/31/97 • Retired mid-August '98 • Estimated Value: ⑤ $12 Rainbow plush, with tongue: Born 10/14/97 • Released mid-August '98 • Retired 3/31/99 • Estimated Value: ⑤ $10

REX THE TYRANNOSAURUS RECOMMENDED

Retired before he was granted a birthday or a poem, this dinosaur's plush is tie-dyed with pink, hot pink, bright magenta, violet, blue, and even orange. Each Rex is a unique work of art. The highly sought-after tie-dyed dinosaur trio of Bronty (page 20), Rex, and Steg (page 78) remains on the wish list of many collectors. Buying them on the secondary market may force collectors to break into the piggy bank, but it's doubtful they'll regret it. Beanie fans should note that Rex, once retired, donated his style number to Lefty the donkey (see page 47).

Born n/a • Released 6/3/95 • Retired 6/15/96 • Estimated Value: ③ $650

RIGHTY THE ELEPHANT HIGHLY RECOMMENDED

Several Beanies share style numbers; Righty shares his with Bronty the brontosaurus (page 20). Another thing Righty shares is his poem, which appears on the tag of his fellow 1996 presidential election commemorative Beanie, Lefty the donkey (page 47). They're the only two Beanies of different styles that have the same poem. Political pundits may think Righty's flag should be on his right side, but that would put the flag's stars too close to his hind end—dishonoring the flag. Some of Righty's tags feature the "sufrace" misspelling. Rightys with an upside-down flag or no flag at all are considered very valuable. The version shown here shows the flag in the correct place and position.

Born 7/4/96 • Released 6/15/96 • Retired 1/1/97 • Estimated Value: 4 $200

RINGO THE RACCOON RECOMMENDED

Ringo's body style is similar to that of Sly the fox (page 71), Stinky the skunk (page 79), and Bucky the beaver (page 21), but his black eye mask (which, as you can see, looks a lot like Fortune the panda's) and his black-ringed tail help him stand out from the crowd. Although Ringo is cute, he was not particularly hard to find as a current, so his retired price may not climb as quickly as some. Then again, most collectors expected Stinky the skunk (the oldest of this lookalike trio) to retire first, so Ringo's surprise retirement may play in his favor, as not many people were rushing to snatch him off the shelves.

Born 7/14/95 • Released 1/7/96 • Retired 9/16/98 • Estimated Value: 3 $75 4 $12 5 $10

ROAM THE BUFFALO

This proud buffalo features a combination of plushes: On his front half and tail, he is covered in dark brown, sculpted nappy plush, but everywhere else the plush is smooth. This combination of plush types is seen on only two other Beanies, Gigi the poodle (pictured on page 37) and Prickles the hedgehog (page 61). Roam's dark brown coloring is accented by the tan stuffed horns that point from his head. Even the most discriminating collectors will enjoy having this bison roam their home!

Born 9/27/98 • Released 9/30/98 • Current • Estimated Value: ❺ $5–7

ROARY THE LION

When Roary made his television debut on the *Today* show a few weeks before the official announcement of his release, he was still nameless. Nonetheless, his appearance sparked great excitement among Beanie collectors nationwide. His long, plush mane, which is similar to Nuts the squirrel's tail (see page 56), is a delight to stroke. Because of the longer plush on the end of Roary's tail, the tail has a seam on the inside, unlike some of the other jungle cats, who have flat tails.

Born 2/20/96 • Released 5/11/97 • Retired 12/31/98 • Estimated Value: ❹ $7 ❺ $7

ROCKET THE BLUE JAY

Rumors about a possible trademark infringement came flying out of left field when Rocket was released in May 1998. The dispute arose due to Major League Baseball's Toronto Blue Jays pitcher, Roger "the Rocket" Clemens. But it's unlikely that Clemens holds a trademark on the name, and the Blue Jays have already used Rocket for a game promotion. This bright blue bird seems to be made for just that purpose! TEENIE BEANIE (THIRD SET)

Born 3/12/97 • Released 5/30/98 • Current • Estimated Value: ❺ $5–7

ROVER THE DOG HIGHLY RECOMMENDED

Red Rover, red Rover, let this Beanie come over! As you can see, Rover bears a strong resemblance to Clifford the Big Red Dog from the popular series of children's books by Norman Bridwell and, for that reason, is highly sought after by fans of the books. The resemblance had also caused many to wonder if Rover would be retired early, but Rover was available for two years before his May 1, 1998, retirement. Rover is also popular as part of the much-loved Beanie dog group. **BEANIE BUDDY**

Born 5/30/96 • Released 6/15/96 • Retired 5/1/98 • Estimated Value: ④ $18 ⑤ $15

SAMMY THE BEAR CUB

The lay down–style bear that had disappeared with Blackie's retirement has been brought back to life with Sammy. This adorable tie-dye bear was created in honor of Chicago Cubs right fielder Sammy Sosa, who, along with Mark McGwire, broke the home run record during the 1998 baseball season. Each Sammy is unique in his colors of blue, pink, yellow, green, orange, and tan, and no doubt collectors will want to end up with a whole den of Sammy bears. As you would guess, Sammy was part of a Ty promotion at Wrigley Field on April 25, 1999.

Born 6/23/98 • Released 1/1/99 • Current • Estimated Value: ⑤ $5–7

SANTA HIGHLY RECOMMENDED

A Ty first! Santa is the first Beanie Baby to be modeled after a human. Santa's most outstanding features are mittens made of the same bright green plush found on Erin the bear (pictured on page 32) and on Pumkin's arms, legs, and leafy stem (see page 62), as well as a nose red enough to make Rudolph proud. Santa's long white beard is similar to the fur found around Stretch the ostrich's neck (see page 79). Santa only remained a current for a few short months before his December 31, 1998, retirement.

Born 12/6/98 • Released 9/30/98 • Retired 12/31/98 • Estimated Value: ♥ $20

SCAT THE CAT

G oing along with the new, floppier body style, Scat's long legs dangle off his body. His plush is the same as Nibbly the rabbit's (page 55) and looks very similar to the 1999 Signature Bear (page 14) and Goatee the mountain goat (page 38)—all released at the same time as Scat. The plush is a mixture of tan and greenish-gray that gives the impression of being a single color when you look at it. Scat, who is not nearly as mangy as his name implies, can be found with two different mouths—either an upward or downward "V" shape. At the moment, neither is more valuable.

Born 5/27/98 • Released 1/1/99 • Current • Estimated Value: ♥ $5–7

SCHWEETHEART THE ORANGUTAN

T y has really gone ape over monkeys! Schweetheart joins Bongo, Congo, Mooch, and Cheeks in the Beanie primate house. This "schweet" orangutan is a sure thing—who could help but go bananas over him? As you can see, Schweetheart's most distinguishing feature is the wild 'do of tan-colored fuzz on top of his head.

Born 1/23/99 • Released 4/11/99 • Current • Estimated Value: ♥ $5–7

SCOOP THE PELICAN

Scoop wasn't one of the more popular Beanies, but since he was included as a Teenie in the second McDonald's set, he'll always be a desirable retired as people search for the original to go with their Teenies. Because of that demand, his value on the secondary market is likely to increase. As seen above, with his huge orange beak, Scoop is an unusual-looking Beanie—one that definitely stands out! **TEENIE BEANIE (SECOND SET)**

Born 7/1/96 • Released 6/15/96 • Retired 12/31/98 • Estimated Value: 🖤 $7 🖤 $7

SCORCH THE DRAGON

A proud successor to Magic the dragon (see page 51), Scorch is made from nappy plush tie-dyed in colors similar to that of the extinct Steg the stegosaurus (pictured on page 78). The multi-hued Scorch features wings of iridescent orange-red, a spine and toes of avocado-green felt, and a tongue of flame-red velveteen ribbon similar to that of Rainbow the chameleon (page 64). Scorch was one of 10 Beanies released in September 1998.

Born 7/31/98 • Released 9/30/98 • Current • Estimated Value: 🖤 $5–7

SCOTTIE THE SCOTTISH TERRIER HIGHLY RECOMMENDED

Scottie is one of only two Beanie Babies to have two birthdays (Freckles the leopard, featured on page 35, is the other). You can find Scottie with a June 3, 1996, birthday as well as a June 15, 1996, birthday. While this is a point of minor interest, collectors should note that there is no additional value associated with either birthday. But if Scottie's hang tag also has the word "always" spelled "slways," that makes him more rare. Scottie is one of just a handful of Beanies with napped fur (see photo) rather than the standard smooth plush.

Born 6/15/96 • Released 6/15/96 • Retired 5/1/98 • Estimated Value: 🖤 $18 🖤 $15

SEAMORE THE SEAL RECOMMENDED

Collectors who found Seamore before her October 1, 1997, retirement, were very lucky indeed. She was extremely difficult to find for months before her retirement. As a result, her post-retirement value skyrocketed well past that of the other Beanies in her retirement class. Finding Seamore in mint condition with clean white plush, as she is in the photo above, can be tricky, but collectors who don't already have this seal should get her now. Her price is sure to continue upward. TEENIE BEANIE (FIRST SET)

Born 12/14/96 • Released 6/25/94 • Retired 10/1/97 • Estimated Value: ❤1 $350 ❤2 $250 ❤3 $150 ❤4 $100

SEAWEED THE OTTER HIGHLY RECOMMENDED

Seaweed can either lie on her back or sit up straight (see photo). In her little otter paws she holds a piece of green felt seaweed (what else!). In this she is unusual, because she is the only Beanie to hold something in her hands. It wasn't a huge surprise when Seaweed retired in mid-September 1998, joining her pal Seamore the seal (see above). Given her scarcity in stores for a couple of months prior to her retirement, Seaweed is bound to increase in value quickly on the secondary market. You "otter" add her to your collection now.

Born 3/19/96 • Released 1/7/96 • Retired 9/19/98 • Estimated Value: ❤3 $75 ❤4 $18 ❤5 $15

SILVER THE GREY TABBY

Hi ho, Silver! Released in April 1999, at the same time as his twin, Amber (page 15), this tabby is gray-striped and is built in the same long-legged body style as Scat the cat (see page 68). Like Amber, Silver has cream-colored paws, inner ears, and lower snout. As the photo shows, he has big blue-rimmed eyes, and a pink nose, whiskers, and mouth. The mouth can be found in either a "V" or an upside-down "V."

Born 2/11/99 • Released 4/21/99 • Current • Estimated Value: ❤5 $5–7

SLIPPERY THE SEAL

Reminiscent of Echo the dolphin, Waves the whale, and Jolly the walrus (pages 31, 87, and 45, respectively), this slippery seal lies on his back. Slippery looks gray, but he's really two colors of gray plush, light and dark. He has mournful little eyes and a V-shaped tail. Released in January 1999, Slippery slipped into the Beanie aquatic family with a splash, replacing the long-retired Seamore the seal (page 70).

Born 1/17/98 • Released 1/1/99 • Current • Estimated Value: ❺ $5–7

SLITHER THE SNAKE RECOMMENDED

This is one snake collectors need not fear. Slither's nearly two-foot length makes him the longest Beanie Baby there is. Finding Slither in any kind of decent condition is quite a feat, though, because his long, red felt tongue often takes the brunt of hard play, and his yellow underside (see photo) is hard to keep clean. Either stretched out to his full length or coiled up and ready to strike, Slither is one of the most desired Beanies around.

Born n/a • Released 6/25/94 • Retired 6/15/95 • Estimated Value: ❶ $1,700 ❷ $1,500 ❸ $1,300

SLY THE FOX HIGHLY RECOMMENDED

Sly sneaked onto the market with a brown belly at first release, but in keeping with its policy of trying to make the Beanies physiologically accurate, Ty soon replaced the brown-bellied version with a white-bellied one (pictured here). The brown-bellied Sly can still be found at moderate prices, but this most likely won't be the case as collectors realize his rarity, especially now that Sly has been retired. It's a good idea for collectors to pick up one of each—if they haven't snuck away yet!

Brown belly: Born 9/12/96 • Released 6/15/96 • Retired 8/6/96 • Estimated Value: ❹ $125 White belly: Born 9/12/96 • Released 8/6/96 • Retired 9/22/98 • Estimated Value: ❹ $10 ❺ $8

SMOOCHY THE FROG

For those who thought Legs the frog was too plain (see page 48), Smoochy should raise no complaints. He's modeled after a tree frog native to Costa Rica and South America. You can tell his origins by his big, bright toes and large eyes (which are red in real life). Tree frogs use these unique features to aid their climbing, but, as you can see, Smoochy benefits from them more in the looks department than anywhere else. Smoochy is a fabulous addition to any Beanie collection. **TEENIE BEANIE (THIRD SET), BEANIE BUDDY**

Born 10/1/97 • Released 12/31/97 • Retired 3/31/99 • Estimated Value: ❺ $7

SNIP THE SIAMESE CAT

In the feline world, the Siamese rule supreme... or so they think. Snip, the Beanie Siamese, imparts this feeling of superiority with her regal bearing and beautiful blue eyes. The darker spots on a Siamese's nose, tail, and paws are called "points," and they come in a variety of colors: chocolate, lilac, seal, and blue (which is actually gray). As you can see, Snip features tan plush with chocolate points, and she was a welcome addition to the popular Beanie cat family.

Born 10/22/96 • Released 1/1/97 • Retired 12/31/98 • Estimated Value: ❹ $7 ❺ $7

SNORT THE BULL RECOMMENDED

When Tabasco the bull was retired, Snort was brought into the Beanie pasture as his replacement. The two Beanies are almost identical, except Snort's hooves (often referred to as "paws") are cream instead of solid red like Tabasco's. (See the photo below and the photo of Tabasco on page 81 for a comparison of their differences.) In addition, the name is the only difference in their poems. Some Snorts were released in Canada in fall 1997 featuring Tabasco's poem, even though the name on the tag read Snort. This little red Beanie bull, who was retired in September 1998, is popular with Chicago Bulls basketball fans as well as with Beanie collectors who want to pair him with Teenie Snort from the original McDonald's collection.

TEENIE BEANIE (FIRST SET), BEANIE BUDDY

Born 5/15/95 • Released 1/1/97 • Retired 9/15/98 • Estimated Value: 🖤 $10 🖤 $8

SNOWBALL THE SNOWMAN HIGHLY RECOMMENDED

Guaranteed not to melt in your hand, Snowball was released and retired quickly along with the 1997 Teddy (featured on page 13). With a body similar to that of Spooky the ghost (see page 76), who was also retired at that time, Snowball usually has a red scarf with white yarn fringe as seen in this photo. But some scarf variations have been reported, including a counterfeit version with green string fringe! Snowball's value should increase dramatically, given his short period of availability. Many collectors never got the chance to see him in stores, but his current secondary-market value is still reasonable enough for most people to consider picking him up.

Born 12/22/96 • Released 10/1/97 • Retired 12/31/97 • Estimated Value: 🖤 $25

SPANGLE THE AMERICAN BEAR

O h, say! Have you seen this American bear? But Spangle isn't exclusive to the United States and, in fact, was found first in the United Kingdom! Spangle is a new-faced bear, but he doesn't have a flag on his chest, as you might expect—he's wearing it all over! His face is white, but the rest of his plush alternates between red-and-white stripes and white stars on a navy blue background. One arm is striped, the other starred. One ear is striped, the other starred. Spangle also sports red and white ribbons around his neck. As you can see, it's an explosion of patriotism!

Born 6/14/99 • Released 4/24/99 • Current • Estimated Value: ⑤ $5–7

SPARKY THE DALMATIAN RECOMMENDED

E ver the helpful fire dog, Sparky let the cat (or should we say "dog"?) out of the bag in early spring 1997 when he was seen sporting "Dotty" tush tags. The rumors that there was a new dog on its way were confirmed when Sparky was retired—due to a trademark dispute with the National Fire Protection Association—and replaced with the almost-identical Dotty. (Sparky's ears and tail are white and spotted, while Dotty's are black. See photos, at left and page 30.) Sparky is still fairly affordable if collectors want to add him to their Beanie kennel.

Born 2/27/96 • Released 6/15/96 • Retired 5/11/97 • Estimated Value: ④ $100

SPEEDY THE TURTLE HIGHLY RECOMMENDED

Speedy, one of the smallest Beanie Babies, is only slightly larger than Trap the mouse (pictured on page 84). Speedy had been on the market quite a while when he was included as one of the Teenie Beanies in the original McDonald's set, prompting renewed interest in him as people ran to get matching Beanie "moms" for their Teenies. As you can see, this avocado green turtle with the brown spotted shell is really very cute. He's still quite affordable as a retired Beanie Baby, and his value has nowhere to go but up. **TEENIE BEANIE (FIRST SET)**

Born 8/14/94 • Released 6/25/94 • Retired 10/1/97 • Estimated Value: ❶ $250
❷ $150 ❸ $75 ❹ $22

SPIKE THE RHINOCEROS RECOMMENDED

Spike's disappearance from retailer shelves in late summer and fall 1997 led to rumors that placed him on the endangered Beanie list. After that, he was spotted more frequently, but he finally retired at the end of 1998. As a formerly hard-to-find release, he'll probably do well on the secondary market; if you see him, herd him into your collection.

Born 8/13/96 • Released 6/15/96 • Retired 12/31/98 • Estimated Value: ❹ $7 ❺ $7

SPINNER THE SPIDER HIGHLY RECOMMENDED

The Beanie Babies collection had been without a spider since Web's retirement in January 1996 and, sadly, only had this little bug for a year's time before he retired in September 1998. Spinner, with his beady red eyes and tiger-striped back, appeared just in time for Halloween 1997. Speaking of his tiger-striped back, collectors will recognize it in this photo as the same plush used for the out-of-production "dark" Stripes the tiger (page 80). In spring 1998, Spinners appeared in the United Kingdom with "Creepy" tush tags. Unfortunately, a new Beanie named "Creepy" has not yet appeared.

Born 10/28/96 • Released 10/1/97 • Retired 9/19/98 • Estimated Value: ❹ $10 ❺ $8

SPLASH THE WHALE

The magnificent Splash, one of the original nine Beanie Babies, displays a striking contrast on his beautiful black-and-white belly. Look for an alternate poem on fourth-generation Splashes. Splash can be distinguished from the other Beanie Babies whale, Waves, because Splash is made in a flatter style than Waves, who appears to be jumping. (See photos, at left and page 87.) Still priced fairly reasonably, Splash is an excellent buy on the secondary market.

Born 7/8/93 • Released 1/8/94 • Retired 5/11/97 • Estimated Value: ❶ $300 ❷ $200 ❸ $125 ❹ $85

SPOOKY THE GHOST

A spooky thing happened on the way to Spooky's retirement. On January 29, 1997, Ty announced that Spooky and Radar the bat (page 63) were retired. The company then turned around the next day and rescinded the announcement, sending collectors into a minor uproar. Spooky's mouth had several variations, but the most important error on this Halloween Beanie was a set of third-generation hang tags on which his name appeared as "Spook." White, as all good ghosts should be, and adorned with a festive orange ribbon, Spooky is the only Beanie ever to have carried his designer's name, Jenna Boldebuck. This attribution is seen only on third-generation tags.

Born 10/31/95 • Released 9/1/95 • Retired 12/31/97 • Estimated Value: ❸ $100 ❹ $30

SPOT THE DOG HIGHLY RECOMMENDED

Spot, one of the original nine Beanie Babies, was initially released without the spot on his back! This spotless Spot is very rare and is highly sought after by serious Beanie collectors. Those searching for the spotless dog should beware—there are counterfeits on the market. The more common, spotted version, shown at right, is quickly becoming scarce, and its value is increasing rapidly. Collectors who don't already own Spot should take him home if they get the chance.

Without spot: Born 1/3/93 • Released 1/8/94 • Retired 4/13/94 • Estimated Value: ❶ $1,700 ❷ $1,500 With spot: Born 1/3/93 • Released 4/13/94 • Retired 10/1/97 • Estimated Value: ❷ $600 ❸ $85 ❹ $33

SPUNKY THE COCKER SPANIEL RECOMMENDED

This cute little blond Cocker Spaniel was an instant hit when he arrived on the market. As you can see, his big, floppy ears are covered with long, wavy plush that is different from all the other Beanie dogs. As part of the very popular dog group of Beanies, and certainly among the cutest, Spunky is a great addition to any collection. TEENIE BEANIE (THIRD SET)

Born 1/14/97 • Released 12/31/97 • Retired 3/31/99 • Estimated Value: ❺ $7

SQUEALER THE PIG HIGHLY RECOMMENDED

Anyone who thinks pigs can't fly should have seen these little piggies do just that as they flew off retailers' shelves! Squealer enjoyed great popularity as a member of the original nine Beanie Babies. Just prior to his expected retirement announcement on May 1, 1998, Squealer became very difficult to find. As a result, Squealer is one of the more valuable retirees from the May 1998 group and is likely to remain so. BEANIE BUDDY

Born 4/23/93 • Released 1/8/94 • Retired 5/1/98 • Estimated Value: ❶ $275 ❷ $175 ❸ $85 ❹ $20 ❺ $18

STEG THE STEGOSAURUS RECOMMENDED

Short and squat, Steg is tie-dyed in tones of yellow, tan, brown, green, and teal. Stegs with large spots of green and teal have proved to be the most popular. As is the case with all the tie-dyed Beanies, each Steg is unique in its pattern. Unlike his dinosaur mates, Bronty and Rex (pages 20 and 64, respectively), who have a tendency to be a little bit limp, Steg is consistently round and plump (see photo). Though he has been the least popular of the three Beanie dinosaurs, Steg is still a very desirable and valuable member of the Beanie family.

Born n/a • Released 6/3/95 • Retired 6/15/96 • Estimated Value: ❸ $625

STILTS THE STORK

Stilts could easily be mistaken for a seagull at first glance, but his long, floppy legs and feet of short orange plush (similar to Pinky the flamingo, page 60, and Stretch the ostrich, opposite page) are a giveaway to his stork heritage. Unlike Pinky, who is immediately noticeable for his shocking pink plush, Stilts features a more subdued white coat and a reddish-orange beak. His wings and tail are proudly edged with black plush. If the popularity of Pinky is any indication, it will be difficult for retailers to keep Stilts stocked on their shelves.

Born 6/16/98 • Released 1/1/99 • Current • Estimated Value: ❺ $5–7

STING THE STINGRAY HIGHLY RECOMMENDED

As beautiful and graceful as a real-life stingray, as shown in this photo, Sting's beautiful blue-and-green tie-dye reflects the colors of the ocean. Beware of seam problems at the place where Sting's tail meets his body. If the stitches are loose, his value could decrease considerably. Sting's unique style and tie-dye patterns are irresistible. His price is fairly reasonable now, but it is likely to go up soon, so pick him up while you can.

Born 8/27/95 • Released 6/3/95 • Retired 1/1/97 • Estimated Value: ❸ $175 ❹ $120

STINGER THE SCORPION

The plainest of the May 30, 1998, releases, Stinger is made from rich cocoa-brown plush that is shinier than the usual plush. His tail is curled, but, as this photo shows, it's a little too floppy to stand up over his back like the tail of a real scorpion. As time goes on, Stinger will become harder to find, so don't get stung by waiting too long to add him to your collection.

Born 9/29/97 • Released 5/30/98 • Retired 9/28/98 • Estimated Value: 5 $7

STINKY THE SKUNK

Stinky has a body style similar to that of Bucky the beaver, Ringo the raccoon, and Sly the fox (pages 21, 65, and 71, respectively), but he is distinguished by the broad white stripe down his back and tail (see at right). Retired along with Ringo and Sly in September 1998, this little stinker has still been fairly easy to find, but he will become more valuable over time.

Born 2/13/95 • Released 6/3/95 • Retired 9/28/98 • Estimated Value: 3 $75 4 $10 5 $7

STRETCH THE OSTRICH

Modeled after Pinky the flamingo (see page 60), Stretch turned out to be the most difficult to find of the January 1998 class of Beanies. As can be seen in this photo, she has long, tan legs and a white ring around her neck, and Beanie collectors like her unusual shape. So far, Stretch doesn't command the high secondary-market prices of some of the other, more rare Beanie Babies, so you should add her to your collection now. TEENIE BEANIE (THIRD SET), BEANIE BUDDY

Born 9/21/97 • Released 12/31/97 • Retired 3/31/99 • Estimated Value: 5 $7

STRIPES THE TIGER RECOMMENDED

The original Stripes is known as "dark" Stripes. His gold color is darker than the newer Stripes (shown here), and his stripes are narrower and closer together. At the same time Stripes got fourth-generation tags, his coat was changed to a lighter gold, almost caramel, color, and his stripes were widened. To figure out which is which, try matching Stripes against Spinner the spider's back, which uses the same fabric as the dark tiger (see page 75). A rare version of the dark Stripes has a more fuzzy plush sewn on his belly. This "fuzzy-belly" Stripes is the most valuable of the three.

Dark, narrow stripes: Born 6/11/95 • Released 1/7/96 • Retired 6/3/96 • Estimated Value: ❸ $225
Light, wide stripes: Born 6/11/95 • Released 6/3/96 • Retired 5/1/98 •
Estimated Value: ❹ $15 ❺ $12

STRUT THE ROOSTER

When Ty encountered a trademark problem with Doodle the rooster (page 29), the company renamed him Strut and kept the same style number and poem. Because Strut wasn't redesigned in any way, owners won't know if they're looking at him or Doodle unless they check the tag. Tie-dyed in bright coral, yellow, hot pink, magenta, and sometimes green (the version shown here is somewhat tame), Strut was retired in March 1999 after less then two years as a current. **TEENIE BEANIE (THIRD SET)**

Born 3/8/96 • Released 7/12/97 • Retired 3/31/99 • Estimated Value: ❹ $7 ❺ $7

SWIRLY THE SNAIL

Y ou'll adore this little slug! Swirly's body is made from pink plush, and he has big blue eyes and two iridescent antennae (made from the same material found on Magic the dragon, Mystic the unicorn, and Halo the angel bear, pages 51, 54, and 40, respectively). But the shell on Swirly's back is something to behold. The outer edge is tie-dyed, while the top swirls are iridescent pink plush. You've got to see him to believe him!

Born 3/10/99 • Released 4/14/99 • Current • Estimated Value: ❺ $5–7

TABASCO THE BULL RECOMMENDED

T y ran into yet another trademark problem with Tabasco, who was retired and quickly followed by his almost-identical twin, Snort (see page 73). As you can see in their photos, Tabasco sports red hooves while Snort has cream hooves. Tabasco's skyrocketing value on the secondary market is legendary, but his rapid ascent has since slowed to match most of the rest of his retiring class. He's still a great Beanie to own—especially for fans of the NBA's Chicago Bulls.

Born 5/15/95 • Released 6/3/95 • Retired 1/1/97 • Estimated Value: ❸ $195 ❹ $130

TANK THE ARMADILLO HIGHLY RECOMMENDED

T ank started out with seven lines of stitching and without the shell that gives armadillos their tanklike look. The second Tank had nine lines of stitching but still no shell. To correct the mistake, Ty finally gave Tank a shell (shown on the far left) and made him smaller and shorter. This Tank's nose lacks the thread nostrils seen on the other two.

Seven lines without shell: Born 2/22/95 • Released 1/7/95 • Retired 1/7/96 • Estimated Value: ❸ $140
Nine lines without shell: Born 2/22/95 • Released 6/3/95 • Retired (unknown) • Estimated Value:
❹ $165 With shell: Born 2/22/95 • Released (unknown) • Retired 10/31/97 • Estimated Value: ❹ $60

TEDDY THE NEW-FACED BEAR `HIGHLY RECOMMENDED`

The new-faced bears can be distinguished from the old-faced bears because of their pouty look and the eyes placed inside the seams on their faces (shown at left). The new-faced brown Teddy is the only one of the colored Teddys that wasn't retired in January 1996. He's also the only Teddy with a poem. The new-faced bears tend to be more popular than the more traditional old-faced bears, but owning any of the bears will make you the envy of other collectors. Violet seems to be the rarest and most popular of the new-faced version. **BEANIE BUDDY (CRANBERRY)**

Brown: Born 11/28/95 • Released 1/7/95 • Retired 10/1/97 • Estimated Value: ❷ $600 ❸ $225 ❹ $90 **Cranberry:** Born n/a • Released 1/7/95 • Retired 1/7/96 • Estimated Value: ❷ $1,500 ❸ $1,250 **Jade:** Born n/a • Released 1/7/95 • Retired 1/7/96 • Estimated Value: ❷ $1,500 ❸ $1,250 **Magenta:** Born n/a • Released 1/7/95 • Retired 1/7/96 • Estimated Value: ❷ $1,500 ❸ $1,250 **Teal:** Born n/a • Released 1/7/95 • Retired 1/7/96 • Estimated Value: ❷ $1,500 ❸ $1,250 **Violet:** Born n/a • Released 1/7/95 • Retired 1/7/96 • Estimated Value: ❷ $1,500 ❸ $1,250

TEDDY THE OLD-FACED BEAR `HIGHLY RECOMMENDED`

Teddy certainly has multiple personalities! These bears are among the most desired of the retired Beanies because of their beautiful colors and because they're bears—the most popular Beanie group. Of the old-faced bears, the brown is the most rare, even though he's the least rare of the new-faced bears. As shown at right, none of the old-faced bears has a ribbon around its neck, so don't worry if you see one without. (Actually, you should beware if you see one *with* a ribbon!) The old-faced bears have pointier noses and eyes set on the outside of the two seams that run from the ears to the nose.

Brown: Born n/a • Released 6/25/94 • Retired 1/7/95 • Estimated Value: ❶ $2,250 ❷ $2,000
Cranberry: Born n/a • Released 6/25/94 • Retired 1/7/95 • Estimated Value: ❶ $1,600 ❷ $1,300
Jade: Born n/a • Released 6/25/94 • Retired 1/7/95 • Estimated Value: ❶ $1,500 ❷ $1,250
Magenta: Born n/a • Released 6/25/94 • Retired 1/7/95 • Estimated Value: ❶ $1,500 ❷ $1,250
Teal: Born n/a • Released 6/25/94 • Retired 1/7/95 • Estimated Value: ❶ $1,500 ❷ $1,250
Violet: Born n/a • Released 6/25/94 • Retired 1/7/95 • Estimated Value: ❶ $1,500 ❷ $1,250

TINY THE CHIHUAHUA

In light of the popularity of a fast-food chain's Chihuahua "spokes-dog," Ty created a Beanie version of this diminutive canine. Made from tan plush, Tiny's standout feature is his huge eyes, which are brown-rimmed and encircled by black plastic that makes them stand out even more. Tiny may be small, but he'll be mighty when it comes to popularity.

Born 9/8/98 • Released 1/1/99 • Current • Estimated Value: ⑤ $5—7

TIPTOE THE MOUSE

Collectors have been clamoring for a new mouse in the collection—especially because most collectors are new to the Beanie scene since Trap was retired, and his hefty price tag prohibits most from owning him. Tiptoe is a wonderfully realistic—and affordable!—replacement. Dressed in brown plush with a long mousy tail, Tiptoe has cream-colored felt ears and, consistent with his name, his toes are also tipped with cream-colored felt.

Born 1/8/99 • Released 4/16/99 • Current • Estimated Value: ⑤ $5—7

TRACKER THE BASSET HOUND

Tracking down this hound, with his sad eyes and long ears, may be a real task for even the most experienced Beanie hunters. Beanie dogs are always popular, but this little fellow may end up being one of the most sought after because collectors find him to be just so darned cute (see photo)! Tracker was introduced on May 30, 1998, along with the rest of the spring 1998 releases. BEANIE BUDDY

Born 6/5/97 • Released 5/30/98 • Current • Estimated Value: ⑤ $5—7

TRAP THE MOUSE RECOMMENDED

T eeny, tiny Trap is the smallest of the Beanie family. As this photo shows, his sleek, light-gray plush is accented by tiny pink feet, nose, ears, and tail, in addition to long, black string whiskers. Hopes ran high among collectors

that Ty would introduce a replacement for Trap that is as cute as he is. Wishes were fulfilled with the release of the very lifelike Tiptoe (see page 83) in April 1999. If you can afford to overlook the retired value on Trap (which is enormous), this mouse is just too adorable to bypass.

Born n/a • Released 6/25/94 • Retired 6/15/95 • Estimated Value: ❤1 $1,300 ❤2 $1,200 ❤3 $1,000

TUFFY THE TERRIER

G iven his terrier background, Tuffy was aptly named, since terriers are probably the most stubborn of the canine family. As seen in this photo, Tuffy's plush is napped rather than smooth like that of the majority of Beanie Babies. Collectors lucky enough to own an early-production Tuffy should check his hang tag to see if his name appears in all capital letters. The all-capital name gives him added value, so keep a leash on him if you have one, especially now that he has been retired.

Born 10/12/96 • Released 5/11/97 • Retired 12/31/98 •
Estimated Value: ❤4 $7 ❤5 $7

TUSK THE WALRUS RECOMMENDED

Tusk can be found with a fourth-generation tag error that spells his name as "Tuck" instead of "Tusk." The "Tuck" version is more rare and, as such, is worth a little more on the secondary market. Don't worry about whether your Tusk's tusks face forward or backward—either is proper and doesn't affect his value one way or the other. Given his older retirement date, Tusk is still well within reach on the secondary market and is a good bet to increase in value in the future.

Born 9/18/95 • Released 1/7/95 • Retired 1/1/97 • Estimated Value: **3** $150 **4** $10

TWIGS THE GIRAFFE HIGHLY RECOMMENDED

As you can see, this plump giraffe with bright orange-and-yellow spots and tiny horns is completely lovable. Many collectors correctly predicted Twigs's May 1, 1998, retirement, and they busily tried to add him to their collections before he disappeared from retailers' shelves. Twigs's long-term value should be strong in the retired market, especially because he is also a "mom" to Teenie Twigs from the second McDonald's Teenie Beanie set. TEENIE BEANIE (SECOND SET), BEANIE BUDDY

Born 5/19/95 • Released 1/7/96 • Retired 5/1/98 • Estimated Value: **3** $75 **4** $15 **5** $12

VALENTINA THE BEAR

Sister to longtime-favorite Valentino, this dusty rose new-faced bear will surely be just as popular. She, too, wears her heart on her chest, but hers is embroidered in white thread. Though you might expect that she would have a white ribbon, in fact, Valentina's ribbon is the same color as her plush. No collection will be complete without this love of a bear.

Born 2/14/98 • Released 1/1/99 • Current •
Estimated Value: **5** $5–7

VALENTINO THE BEAR HIGHLY RECOMMENDED

Valentino, a longtime favorite, has seen his last Valentine's Day as a current. He hung around for three February holidays, fueling speculation that Ty would release a new Beanie in his place the next year, and, voila, they did! Valentina (page 85) appeared in his place for the 1999 holiday. Valentino with fifth-generation hang tags is the hardest to find, especially since these were among the tags that misspelled "origiinal" and "suface." This white bear with the red "I love you" heart resides in the Baseball Hall of Fame in Cooperstown, New York—a memento of the day David Wells of the New York Yankees pitched a perfect game. Valentino was given to fans as part of a Beanie Babies promotion at Yankee Stadium that day.

Born 2/14/94 • Released 1/7/95 • Retired 12/31/98 • Estimated Value: **2** $200
3 $85 **4** $18 **5** $15

VELVET THE PANTHER RECOMMENDED

As this photo shows, Velvet's pinky-peach nose is a striking contrast to the rest of her silky, all-black body. Although she's been retired since October 1997, Velvet was easy to find in stores just before her retirement, so she can still be found on the secondary market for a reasonable price. If you don't have her yet, get her while you can. She may become more difficult to find over time, and her price will reflect it.

Born 12/16/95 • Released 6/3/95 • Retired 10/1/97 • Estimated Value: **3** $75 **4** $18

WADDLE THE PENGUIN

Short and stout, this little penguin looks like he's wearing a tuxedo, doesn't he? Waddle is finding favor with collectors because he is a "mom" to the Teenie Beanie Waddle, found in the second McDonald's promotion, and a Beanie Buddy as well. Due to the many collectors still searching for this well-dressed penguin, his value on the secondary market is likely to increase steadily. TEENIE BEANIE (SECOND SET), BEANIE BUDDY

Born 12/19/95 • Released 6/3/95 • Retired 5/1/98 • Estimated Value: **3** $75 **4** $15 **5** $12

WAVES THE WHALE

Waves could never totally replace Splash, the original whale (page 76), but he makes a place of his own in Beanie history. He and Echo the dolphin were originally released wearing each other's tags, causing confusion among collectors (see page 31). Eventually the tag mistake was rectified, and the mistagged versions of both Beanies are slightly more valuable than those with the correct tags—especially now that both are retired. Waves's relatively short life as a current should mean strong secondary-market values for him as a retired.

Born 12/8/96 • Released 5/11/97 • Retired 5/1/98 • Estimated Value: **4** $15 **5** $12

Web the Spider Recommended

The Beanie Babies collection went almost two years without a spider after Web was retired and before Spinner (page 75) was introduced. From the top, Web at first looks rather dull and unimaginative, with a black plush body, head, and legs, and little black eyes (see photo). But turn this arachnid over and you'll see a bright red stomach! Web's legs have a seam from tip to mid-leg. This seam makes his legs look jointed; when he is placed on his belly, his legs can be bent to look like he's ready to scamper away.

Born n/a • Released 6/25/94 • Retired 1/7/96 • Estimated Value: ❶ $1,100 ❷ $1,000 ❸ $900

Weenie the Dachshund Highly Recommended

With little bug eyes and ears that fly out to the side, Weenie always looks alarmed. Weenie has been a consistently popular Beanie ever since his introduction, even though he never distinguished himself with a notorious tag error or redesign. Ty must have realized they had a real "wiener" on their hands! Bones the dog and Weenie were the oldest of the Beanie dogs, so their May 1, 1998, retirement wasn't a big surprise to collectors.

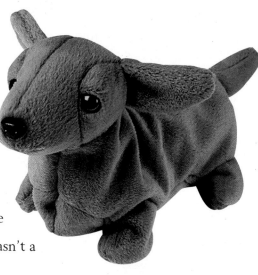

Born 7/20/95 • Released 1/7/96 • Retired 5/1/98 • Estimated Value: ❸ $75 ❹ $20 ❺ $18

WHISPER THE DEER

Shhhhhh! If you're very quiet, you might be able to get this shy little deer to come home with you. Styled similarly to the May 1, 1998-retired Twigs the giraffe (pictured on page 85), Whisper features a white-spotted back and large, sweetly appealing ears. Some collectors had hoped for more original styling, but they weren't able to resist fawning over her for long.

Born 4/5/97 • Released 5/30/98 • Current • Estimated Value: 🖤 $5–7

WISE THE OWL HIGHLY RECOMMENDED

You'll be wise indeed if you add this owl to your collection quickly! With "Class of 1998" imprinted on his mortarboard, Wise was sure to be a quick retiree. Rumors of retirement due to a trademark infringement with the Wise Potato Chip company seem to be unfounded, even though they use an owl for their mascot as well. Wise's days were already numbered (with his 1998 graduation date), so he'd have flown the coop by the time the case could go to court.

Born 5/31/97 • Released 5/30/98 • Retired 12/31/98 • Estimated Value: 🖤 $11

WISER THE OWL

Wiser the owl follows Wise, who represented the class of 1998. Wiser's gray-striped plush has white accents, and he wears a mortarboard and tassel—just like Wise, but this one reads "Class of 1999," instead. You don't have to be a Beanie expert or a fortune teller to spot the trend here.... Will the Class of 2000 be the Wisest of all? Wise collectors will snap Wiser up soon, as it's practically a given that he'll be retired sometime this year.

Born 6/4/99 • Released 4/22/99 • Current • Estimated Value: 🖤 $5–7

WRINKLES THE BULLDOG HIGHLY RECOMMENDED

This tan-and-white bulldog will give you a serious case of puppy love thanks to a face that just begs to be picked up and petted. Constructed similarly to Pugsly the Pug dog (pictured on page 62), Wrinkles gets his name from his most obvious characteristic: the wrinkles that are stitched in from his wide muzzle and forehead all the way down his back (see photo). Now that Wrinkles is retired, he is more sought-after than ever.

Born 5/1/96 • Released 6/15/96 • Retired 9/22/98 • Estimated Value: ❹ $10 ❺ $8

ZERO THE PENGUIN HIGHLY RECOMMENDED

Dressed to withstand cold winter temperatures with his red stocking cap, Zero is very similar to his penguin predecessor, Waddle (see page 87). Zero's beak and feet are bright orange, and, as you can see, his beak is more cone-shaped than Waddle's. He was introduced in fall 1998—just in time for collectors to start thinking about winter—and retired just as quickly!

Born 1/2/98 • Released 9/30/98 • Retired 12/31/98 •
Estimated Value: ❺ $15

ZIGGY THE ZEBRA

Ziggy had a fabric change in fall 1997, when his stripes were made a little wider and no longer branched off into "Y" shapes. This is the version that is pictured at right. The older Ziggy is being stalked by Beanie predators and has been worth a little more than the later version, but with his retirement taking place only six months after the redesign, this may not remain the case for long. Both versions are nice additions to a collection, because Ziggy is the only zebra in the Beanie Babies zoo.

Born 12/24/95 • Released 6/3/95 • Retired 5/1/98 • Estimated Value: ❸ $75 ❹ $15 ❺ $10

ZIP THE BLACK CAT

Zip has gone through the same design changes as Nip (page 55). The earliest Zip had a rounded head, white muzzle and belly, and pink ears and whiskers. The second Zip, the rarest version, had an all-black face and belly. The latest Zip (shown) is smaller, with white ears and paws, and is "mom" to Teenie Zip from the second McDonald's promotion. TEENIE BEANIE (SECOND SET)

White face and belly: Born 3/28/94 • Released 1/7/95 • Retired 1/7/96 •
Estimated Value: ❷ $375 ❸ $300 All black: Born 3/29/94 • Released 1/7/96 •
Retired 3/10/96 • Estimated Value: ❸ $850 White paws: Born 3/28/94 • Released 3/10/96 •
Retired 5/1/98 • Estimated Value: ❸ $200 ❹ $25 ❺ $20

Beanie Babies Checklist

- ❏ 1997 Teddy
- ❏ 1998 Teddy
- ❏ 1999 Signature Bear
- ❏ Ally the alligator
- ❏ Almond the bear
- ❏ Amber the gold tabby
- ❏ Ants the anteater
- ❏ Baldy the eagle
- ❏ Batty the bat
  - ❏ brown
  - ❏ tie-dye
- ❏ Beak the kiwi bird
- ❏ Bernie the St. Bernard
- ❏ Bessie the cow
- ❏ Blackie the bear
- ❏ Blizzard the tiger
- ❏ Bones the dog
- ❏ Bongo the monkey
- ❏ Britannia the bear
- ❏ Bronty the brontosaurus
- ❏ Brownie the bear
- ❏ Bruno the terrier
- ❏ Bubbles the fish
- ❏ Bucky the beaver
- ❏ Bumble the bee
- ❏ Butch the bull terrier
- ❏ Canyon the cougar
- ❏ Caw the crow
- ❏ Cheeks the baboon
- ❏ Chilly the polar bear
- ❏ Chip the calico cat
- ❏ Chocolate the moose
- ❏ Chops the lamb
- ❏ Claude the crab
- ❏ Congo the gorilla
- ❏ Coral the fish
- ❏ Crunch the shark

- ❏ Cubbie the bear
- ❏ Curly the bear
- ❏ Daisy the cow
- ❏ Derby the horse
  - ❏ coarse mane
  - ❏ fine mane
  - ❏ white star
  - ❏ fuzzy mane
- ❏ Digger the crab
  - ❏ orange
  - ❏ red
- ❏ Doby the Doberman
- ❏ Doodle the rooster
- ❏ Dotty the Dalmatian
- ❏ Early the robin
- ❏ Ears the brown rabbit
- ❏ Echo the dolphin
- ❏ Eggbert the hatching chick
- ❏ Erin the bear
- ❏ Eucalyptus the koala
- ❏ Ewey the lamb
- ❏ Fetch the Golden Retriever
- ❏ Flash the dolphin
- ❏ Fleece the lamb
- ❏ Flip the white cat
- ❏ Floppity the lilac bunny
- ❏ Flutter the butterfly
- ❏ Fortune the panda
- ❏ Freckles the leopard
- ❏ Fuzz the bear
- ❏ Garcia the bear
- ❏ Germania the bear
- ❏ Gigi the Poodle
- ❏ Glory the bear
- ❏ Goatee the mountain goat
- ❏ Gobbles the turkey
- ❏ Goldie the goldfish

- ❑ Goochy the jellyfish
- ❑ Gracie the swan
- ❑ Grunt the razorback
- ❑ Halo the angel bear
- ❑ Happy the hippo
  - ❑ gray
  - ❑ lavender
- ❑ Hippie the tie-dye bunny
- ❑ Hippity the mint bunny
- ❑ Hissy the snake
- ❑ Hoot the owl
- ❑ Hope the praying bear
- ❑ Hoppity the rose bunny
- ❑ Humphrey the camel
- ❑ Iggy the iguana
- ❑ Inch the inchworm
  - ❑ felt antennae
  - ❑ yarn antennae
- ❑ Inky the octopus
  - ❑ pink
  - ❑ tan, no mouth
  - ❑ tan, with mouth
- ❑ Jabber the parrot
- ❑ Jake the mallard duck
- ❑ Jolly the walrus
- ❑ Kicks the soccer bear
- ❑ Kiwi the toucan
- ❑ Knuckles the pig
- ❑ Kuku the cockatoo
- ❑ Lefty the donkey
- ❑ Legs the frog
- ❑ Libearty the bear
- ❑ Lizzy the lizard
  - ❑ blue
  - ❑ tie-dyed
- ❑ Loosy the goose
- ❑ Lucky the ladybug
  - ❑ 7 spots
  - ❑ 11 spots
  - ❑ 21 spots
- ❑ Luke the black lab
- ❑ Mac the cardinal
- ❑ Magic the dragon
- ❑ Manny the manatee
- ❑ Maple the bear
- ❑ Mel the koala
- ❑ Millennium the bear
- ❑ Mooch the spider monkey
- ❑ Mystic the unicorn
  - ❑ coarse mane
  - ❑ fine mane
  - ❑ iridescent horn
  - ❑ rainbow mane
- ❑ Nana the monkey
- ❑ Nanook the Husky
- ❑ Neon the seahorse
- ❑ Nibbler the rabbit
- ❑ Nibbly the rabbit
- ❑ Nip the gold cat
  - ❑ all gold
  - ❑ white face and belly
  - ❑ white paws
- ❑ Nuts the squirrel
- ❑ Osito the Mexican bear
- ❑ Patti the platypus
  - ❑ deep fuchsia
  - ❑ fuchsia
  - ❑ magenta
  - ❑ raspberry
- ❑ Paul the walrus
- ❑ Peace the bear
- ❑ Peanut the elephant
  - ❑ light blue
  - ❑ royal blue
- ❑ Pecan the bear
- ❑ Peking the panda
- ❑ Pinchers the lobster
- ❑ Pinky the flamingo
- ❑ Pouch the kangaroo
- ❑ Pounce the cat
- ❑ Prance the cat
- ❑ Prickles the hedgehog
- ❑ Princess the bear
- ❑ Puffer the puffin
- ❑ Pugsly the Pug
- ❑ Pumkin' the pumpkin
- ❑ Punchers the lobster
- ❑ Quackers the duck
  - ❑ with wings
  - ❑ without wings
- ❑ Radar the bat
- ❑ Rainbow the chameleon

- ❏ Rex the tyrannosaurus
- ❏ Righty the elephant
- ❏ Ringo the raccoon
- ❏ Roam the buffalo
- ❏ Roary the lion
- ❏ Rocket the blue jay
- ❏ Rover the dog
- ❏ Sammy the bear cub
- ❏ Santa
- ❏ Scat the cat
- ❏ Schweetheart the orangutan
- ❏ Scoop the pelican
- ❏ Scorch the dragon
- ❏ Scottie the Scottish Terrier
- ❏ Seamore the seal
- ❏ Seaweed the otter
- ❏ Silver the grey tabby
- ❏ Slippery the seal
- ❏ Slither the snake
- ❏ Sly the fox
  - ❏ brown belly
  - ❏ white belly
- ❏ Smoochy the frog
- ❏ Snip the Siamese cat
- ❏ Snort the bull
- ❏ Snowball the snowman
- ❏ Spangle the American bear
- ❏ Sparky the Dalmatian
- ❏ Speedy the turtle
- ❏ Spike the rhinoceros
- ❏ Spinner the spider
- ❏ Splash the whale
- ❏ Spooky the ghost
- ❏ Spot the dog
  - ❏ with spot
  - ❏ no spot
- ❏ Spunky the Cocker Spaniel
- ❏ Squealer the pig
- ❏ Steg the stegosaurus
- ❏ Stilts the stork
- ❏ Sting the stingray
- ❏ Stinger the scorpion
- ❏ Stinky the skunk
- ❏ Stretch the ostrich
- ❏ Stripes the tiger
  - ❏ dark
- ❏ light
- ❏ Strut the rooster
- ❏ Swirly the snail
- ❏ Tabasco the bull
- ❏ Tank the armadillo
  - ❏ nine lines
  - ❏ nine lines, no shell
  - ❏ seven lines, no shell
- ❏ Teddy the new-faced bear
  - ❏ brown
  - ❏ cranberry
  - ❏ jade
  - ❏ magenta
  - ❏ teal
  - ❏ violet
- ❏ Teddy the old-faced bear
  - ❏ brown
  - ❏ cranberry
  - ❏ jade
  - ❏ magenta
  - ❏ teal
  - ❏ violet
- ❏ Tiny the Chihuahua
- ❏ Tiptoe the mouse
- ❏ Tracker the Basset Hound
- ❏ Trap the mouse
- ❏ Tuffy the terrier
- ❏ Tusk the walrus
- ❏ Twigs the giraffe
- ❏ Valentina the bear
- ❏ Valentino the bear
- ❏ Velvet the panther
- ❏ Waddle the penguin
- ❏ Waves the whale
- ❏ Web the spider
- ❏ Weenie the Dachshund
- ❏ Whisper the deer
- ❏ Wise the owl
- ❏ Wiser the owl
- ❏ Wrinkles the Bulldog
- ❏ Zero the penguin
- ❏ Ziggy the zebra
- ❏ Zip the black cat
  - ❏ all black
  - ❏ white face and belly
  - ❏ white paws